FLOURISHING COMMUNITIES
Insights from Ambedkar and Bible

FLOURISHING COMMUNITIES

Insights from Ambedkar and Bible

Monodeep Daniel

&

Samuel John Shekhar

2021

Flourishing Communities: Insights from Ambedkar and Bible - Published by the Indian Society for Promoting Christian Knowledge (ISPCK), Post Box 1585, Kashmere Gate, Delhi-110006.

Online order: http://ispck.org.in/book.php

Also available on amazon.in

ISBN: 978-81-947592-5-6

Laser typeset by

ISPCK, Post Box 1585, 1654, Madarsa Road, Kashmere Gate, Delhi-110006 • *Tel:* 23866323

e-mail: ashish@ispck.org.in • ella@ispck.org.in
website: www.ispck.org.in

Contents

Foreword
Flourishing Communities:
A Hope for Fragile People

Competition and conflict among communities are regularly reported in the news. Routinely clips of such news are circulated on the public and private media channels. In contrast flourishing communities do not compete or clash, instead they engage in *sharing* and *caring* of their members and also of the rest. In other words a community experiences flourishing when its members share among themselves values and interests and a common purpose. So what is the result of such sharing? It is just this that instead of being stifled, a social space is created for all people—diverse and distinct—to enjoy dignity, live in security, and to have the *privilege* to speak their minds and *opportunities* to develop their capabilities. It allows people to *participate* in the social, economic, cultural, political and cultural life of the community. This brings about changes in the wider society to become more just, compassionate, tolerant, inclusive and sustainable.

In the Indian context, I feel that we can identify at least four hurdles for communities to flourish. These hurdles which make people feeble and fragile emerge due to the curse of caste system. However, this must not drive us to despair. In all fragile conditions we must promote flourishing communities seriously. These issues pertain to caste inequality, unfair distribution of natural resources, relentless social conflicts and narrow-mindedness. Let us discuss each of them under appropriate headings below.

Manipulation of Society

I must draw attention to the fact that the whole system of caste has manipulated social arrangement on the principle of graded inequality. It does not apologize for doing so because long before anyone could challenge it in the antiquity, the caste system was made a sacred order. This casteist inequality is the hallmark of Brahmanism and is reinforced by all means. It is reinforced politically by graded inequality, economically by fixation of occupation and socially by fixity of birth.

In our present times inequality is visible in the "gated residential colonies" which encourages social segregation of economic classes. It must be admitted that the economically progressive classes are mostly the dominant castes. Fortunately in the urban areas the castes among the middle and lower-middle classes and due to the presence of minorities in the neighborhood are not always identifiable. But the fact is that people know their caste even if they don't follow its rules rigorously.

Attention should also be drawn to the problem of gender inequality. In the Indian social context gender inequality emerges from casteist form of patriarchy and so in its flavor it is distinct from its western counterpart. Admittedly, it only complicates the unequal social order further. This social complication has been underscored in this study, that despite the subjugation of women under males across the castes, the Brahmin woman is superior to Kshatriya male and so on down the descending line of caste purity. It is to say that women are subordinate and superordinate to the males at the same time. This is a most extraordinary arrangement of using women, despite subordinating them, to suppress others. However, this does not condone their subordination. Whatever its strange feature due to the caste system, patriarchy is a nuisance to reckon with.

Monopoly over Resources

It is no secret that caste system comes into operation when State policy is unclear; for instance, in the distribution of resources among the refugees in a flood. The exploding population in India which crossing 1.38 billion (138 crores) is causing serious shortages of natural resources i.e. energy, fresh water, fuel, raw-materials and food. These are not distributed in a just and sustainable manner. Most of the population does not get adequate electricity or fresh water supply through the day. It is expected that competition for scarce resources will become more intense. In this competition the dominant castes being the most powerful and best placed players will grab the biggest shares. If it were a mere case of their walking away with larger piece of cake there would still be hope for others to have the rest; the dismal fact is that the members of the powerful castes have taken control of the public resources and monopolized it to their own advantage. Admittedly this monopoly is increasing the case of unfair distribution of resources.

Relentless Nature of Conflicts

We are aware that conflicts have been going on since the antiquity of the Indian history. It was between Aryans and Nags, Dikku and Adivasi, and Brahmanism and Buddhism. Conflicts were initiated by the Aryans, Brahmans and Dikkus to subjugate the Nags, Buddhists and Adivasis. The aim to vanquish the later was to control the seven sources of fresh water, namely, 1. Indus-Sarasvati; 2. Ganga-Yamuna; 3. Brahmaputra; 4. Narmada-Tapti; 5. Krishna-Godavari; 6. Cauvery; and 7. the Five Rivers of Punjab. But the conquest of the fresh water sources was not profitable in itself unless they turned the vanquished people into slaves to till, irrigate and cultivate the land, and retrieve precious minerals and metals from it. These people have become Dalits who constitute more than seventeen percent of the Indian population.

During the course of history Brahmanism forged caste system which gradually organized the society, as Dr Ambedkar had pointed out, on the structure of graded inequality, fixity of occupation and fixation of birth. It is a form of structured violence pushing people to live in a state of perpetual social conflict.

Utter Selfishness

Casteism breeds self-centeredness in each person. Individuals become utterly selfish and restrict their interest to preserve their caste purity and follow caste injunction particularly in the case of marriage. Individuals consciously connect to their family and in the widest orbit to their *jati, gotra* and *Varna* which bestows on them their identity and consciousness. Beyond this there is little interest in the welfare and progress of the rest who belong to different castes, languages, religions or regions. Self-centeredness not only adversely affects the flourishing of individuals but it is also a threat to national and social security.

As the result of manipulation, monopolization and conflict the fabric of society which should be cohesive and harmonious, has become fragile. It has made the Indian society infertile to cultivate a robust national culture. Had it been properly cultivated, society would have flourished. It would have included all diversities—cultural, religious, lingual and ethnic. Conversely, the fragile society had made human beings feeble.

In the present social context of manipulation, monopoly and conflict, individuals are caught in the vicious net of caste-based segregation, untouchability, discrimination and poverty. Dalit and Adivasi seem to have reached the dead end of the tunnel with no visible route to escape. But even if the situation looks grim, there can be no question of surrender. The prospect to form *Flourishing Communities* is the light at the end of the tunnel. It is the unifying vision of Dalit and Adivasi who like any other people are social creatures capable of overcoming social and economic problems by drawing on the power of community rather than simply depending on individual effort. They can pursue their goals and achieve their aims by working together as opposed to striving for personal self-interest. As John Donne (1571-1631) wrote,

> No man is an island entire of itself;
> every man is a piece of the Continent, a part of the main ...
> any man's death diminishes me, because I am involved in Mankind; and
> therefore never send to know for whom the bell tolls;
> it tolls for thee.

This recovery of focus on community-life offers hope for individuals who hitherto have been made feeble due to fragile social conditions. Only a flourishing community can empower its individual members when the prospects of prosperity of the wider society seems fragile.

I am happy that Revd. Samuel John Shekhar and Dr. Monodeep Daniel have brought out this book on *Flourishing*

Communities under the Delhi Brotherhood Society's *Centre for Dalit/Subaltern Studies.* The original material were the two Bible Studies conducted by Revd. Shekhar who represented the CNI at the pre-assembly meet of the "Council for World Mission" held in Kolkata in 2019. In the first study he laid down the *foundations* of flourishing communities and in the second its functional *principles.* Both were deduced from the biblical sources. To this basic material Dr. Daniel supplemented more resources to give wider perspective and greater depth with economy of words so that this book becomes inspiring, handy and affordable for people. My hope is that this study on the concept of *Flourishing Communities* will help the readers to analyze afresh social problems emerging from caste system.

Revd. Solomon George
Director
Delhi Brotherhood Society
July 25, 2020

Preface

After generations of people who experienced excesses of industrial capitalism on the one hand and communism on the other, and then the failure of communists to establish public equality, serious attempts were made to reclaim the social dimension of life. Keeping in view that societal changes take long time to achieve the desired goals of socialism, a way forward is to recover the role of communities. It is an accepted fact that individuals find opportunities to develop their potentials and gain respect within their communities. In the nineteenth century utopian socialists such as Charles Fourier and Robert Owen experimented in communal living. Fourier motivated people to start *Phalasteries* which were model communities of about 1,800 members. Owen also initiated several experimental communities, out of which *New Harmony Indiana* (1824-29) became well known.

However, the most durable experiment has been the *Kibbutz* community in rural Israel. The communities were collectively owned by their members and administered on cooperative system. Eventually the communitarian emphasis of *Kibbutz* got diluted and it adapted itself to the changing social context. In Africa and Asia there was a rediscovery of community values from their preindustrial and traditional past. If their traditional communitarian life was reinstituted it could offer human beings genuine emancipation and fulfillment. This directly challenged the individualism of the western thought.

In the Christian tradition, the religious communities came into existence since the third century after St. Anthony (251-366) established himself in the Egyptian deserts. He is regarded as the father of Christian monasticism because after him arose a grand monastic movement in the Christian world. Four Rules of Life were set out for the monks and nuns in religious communities, namely, the Rules of St Benedict, St Basil, St Augustine and St Francis. They are all similar but also distinct from each other.

In recent times more exciting initiatives were taken to set up communities. We have seen three examples above, namely, *Phalasteries, New Harmony* and *Kibbutz*. These *experimental* communities were ideologically propelled. However, the example of *L'Arche*, a community of people with different mental behavior, started in 1964 by Jean Vanier in France is an example of *intentional* community. He wrote,

> "Every community must have a Charter, which specifies clearly why its members are living together and what is expected of each of them. It also means that before a community begins, its members should take time to prepare for living together and clarify their aims."

Other such examples of *intentional* communities are the religious communities like those of Mother Teresa's *Missionaries of Charity* Kolkata, and Bishop B.F. Westcott's *The Brotherhood of the Ascended Christ* Delhi. There are so many of them all over the world. Intentional aspect creates a very strong bonding of feelings among the members of the community.

There is a recovery of the idea of *community* to empower people with inspiration to create circumstances for their own advancement within the environment in their communities. Jean Vanier knew this way back in 1964 that the modern society of his times was the product of disintegration of more or less natural or familial groupings. People were afraid, uncertain, and had largely shut themselves up, in their houses. But the fact was that they needed companions and friends with whom they could share their lives, their visions and their ideals; in short they needed community.

This book is an exploration in this area which we now call *Flourishing Communities*. The opposite of this is the *fragile* condition from which Dalit and Adivasi have to be emancipated. It is towards this end that the six chapters including the two bible studies lay biblical foundations and principles for community life to flourish in the midst of a society which is ridden with casteism, regionalism and religious bigotry. Flourishing Community is the hope for every oppressed person to progress in life.

Along with my co-author Revd Samuel John Shekhar, we want to end this piece with a note of gratitude to Revd Fr Solomon George, Director of Delhi Brotherhood Society, a journalist and a political activist, for writing the Foreword to this book and a very big thanks to Kirk-in-Actie in The Netherlands for providing the necessary funds for the publication of this book, which was written and completed during the COVID-19 lockdown period 2020 in the National Capital Territory of Delhi.

Monodeep Daniel

Chapter 1

Ambedkar's Insights to Flourish

The theme of this study is *Flourishing Communities*. The global culture is now post-modern with revolutionary progress in space and media technology. It is the age of advanced and fast communication. However, the most crucial hallmark of the postmodernism is the "turn of relationships." Stanley J. Grenz in his essay *Ecclesiology* highlights the problem of loneliness of individuals in the postmodern society. Very different from late modern mind-set where fulfilment was seen in terms of work, economics, privacy and material progress, Grenz states that

> "Postmodernists acknowledges today that humans are fundamentally social creatures, and therefore, that the emptiness which individuals sense can never be filled by the abundance of possessions but only in relationship with others." [VK 2003:252].

From Christian perspective this focus on relationship is correct. Granted that human quest for wholeness can finally find fulfilment through relationship with God alone, nevertheless belonging to God involves belonging to God's community. That is why membership in the fellowship of Christ's disciples i.e. the church, is regarded as important. This social belonging to the church has to be active and participatory of all God's people [VK 2003:253]. For the sake of clarity we will study about community in sections below.

What is a Community?

The buzz-word in the recent years is *community.* Godson Jacob, a young theologian of Indian origin, writes "Community is an existential and social fact which becomes a lived experience only in relation to fellow beings" [JG 2019:2] *Gemeinschaft* and *Gesellschaft.* The root of the word community is French *comunete* which comes from the Latin *communitas* and *communis,* denoting things *shared in common.* In fact socialization of a child begins within the primordial bonds of family and community which is its extended form. It must be further admitted that community and society are connected and have similar features but they are different entities. Community primarily involves love, which supports its members by offering dignity and preserves moral responsibility, whereas society involves contract i.e. a web of relationships involving institutions like marriage, or associations like business and judiciary to meet various human needs of security, trade, livelihood, and family life. Let me cite Godson Jacob here,

> "Human beings in general are divided into two: communities and societies. They are the two modes of social order and structure. Ferdinand Tonnies employs two concepts *Gemeinschaft* and *Gesellschaft.* It is approximately translated as community and society respectively. He examines it by viewing the human volition of which he distinguished two types: *wesenswill* (natural will) and *kurwille* (rational will). *Gemeinschaft* refers to the community of feeling that results from likeness and from shared life experiences. In them, individuals consider other individuals, as end in themselves, which they know each other personally, create emotional bonds through frequent face-to-face interaction and mutually participate in each other's lives. This action is based on natural will.

Gesellschaft or society on the other hand, connotes a completely different setting where people live in large, densely populated area; they have diverse values, roles and tradition. Their relation in public life is more on a contractual basis. This action is moreover on a rational will." [JG 2019: 11].

A society will contain several communities which are social subsystems in a biosphere and whose members are bound in daily transactions as they exchange goods and services. In the first half of twentieth century small communities had emerged as significant players in the industrial society which saw a surge in urbanisation and mushrooming of suburban sprawls. Major studies were published in connection with life in metropolitans. The first such study was published in 1915 by Rober E. Park under the title *The City: Suggestions for investigation of Human Behaviour in the Urban Environment* [EB Vol-20 1973:790].

What Robert Stebbins, professor emeritus in sociology in the Calgary University Canada, describes as features of a society is equally applicable to describe a community as well. It has three features: *firstly* that it is relatively self-sufficient; *secondly* that its members largely maintain direct or indirect contact with each other; and *thirdly* they share a common culture which functions as the basis for their communication. Culture is federally understood as the shared language, beliefs, goals, artefacts and experiences that combine together to form a unique pattern. Every human is born in a community, and shares the common life of community, whether large or small. In every way culture is woven in the community through the warp and woof of human adaptations to their environment.

Forging of Community

A community is forged or formed by a group of people or individuals who come together in an expectation of a special relationship which is voluntary, yet defining. They share certain values, services, institutions, interest or geographical proximity keeping a spirit of belonging and mutual dependence.

Generally any community is forged by social bonding. This bonding among its members is reinforced by their intention. If the intention is to grow together, then it has to be by sharing a common identity created by a set shared beliefs, practices and roles. In practice it is to share one's assets to meet the needs of other members. With these defining feature innumerable types of communities have been forged in a society which are both religious and secular in nature.

According to contemporary sociologists, several crucial characteristics can define the functioning of all communities. To these we will turn our attention in the following section of our study.

Three Features of Community

Stanley J. Grenz, a post-modernist theologian, spells out the concept of community in contemporary thought in his essay *Ecclesiology* (2003). He holds that *first* of all a community consists of a group of people who are conscious that they share a similar frame of reference, which inclines them to view the world in a similar manner, to *read* the world through similar glasses, and to construct the symbolic world they inhabit using similar linguistic and symbolic building materials, even if the members of the community are not of one mind as to what their various world-constructing symbols mean. *Second*, operative in all communities is a group focus that evokes a shared sense of group identity among the members, whose attention is thereby directed toward the group. Group identity, which is fostered in part by the belief that the participants engage in a common task, nurtures a type of solidarity among the members. Moreover, rather than necessitating unanimity and uniformity of opinion among group members, group focus entails a shared interest in participating in an outgoing discussion as to what constitutes the identity of the group. A *third* major characteristic of a community is the "person focus" that balances its group orientation. Insofar as its members draw their personal identity from the community, the group is a crucial factor in forming its participants. This third aspect leads to what for the purposes of ecclesiology constitutes the central function of community, its role in identity formation [VK 2003:253].

Grenz in the above excerpt garners three features of community from various sociological studies. *One*, that members of the community share similar symbols; *two*, they share a similar identity; and *three*, it functions as a school of formation for its members. A community operates on these three features. Let us study each of these below.

Community Members Shares Similar Symbols

Stories or narratives constitute important symbols for, community members. As far as history, religion and philosophy are concerned, there are no mega narratives in postmodern society anymore. Postmodernism is an age of relativity and pluralism. All stories or theologies or multiple moral codes which carry symbolic power and value are equally valid. However, each community has its own narrative. Philosophers like Alasdair MacIntyre have linked the understanding of community with the postmodernist changes in perspective. He examines community in the light of the narrative theory. In this line of thinking human-beings are storytellers who create their symbols of identity by the telling of a personal narrative, in accordance with what *makes sense* of life. These personal stories are tied up with the larger group story i.e. the narrative of a community [VK 2003:254]. This narrative works as a symbol to keep the community bonded into a cohesive whole.

Community Members Shares Similar Identity

George Stroud explored the connection of personal identity with community in a comprehensive way. According to him identity of a person emerges with the use of specific events selected from his/her past to interpret the significance of one's whole life. Personal identity is not created merely from the factual data or chronicle of the events of one's life; instead it requires an *interpretive scheme* that provides the *plot* through which the chronicle makes sense. This scheme arises from one's social context or tradition. It cannot be derived from the data of one's own life. For this reason Stroud concluded that personal identity can never be a private reality but has a communal element; it is shaped by the community in which the person is a participant. Such a community contributes to the formation of the *self* by mediating the common narrative necessary for the formation of personal identity. Hence, members of a community share a common identity.

A Community Functions as a School of Formation

The identity-conferring aspect of community leads to what sociologists such as Robert Nisbet and Robert Perrin level as a *reference group*. In other words it is "the social group to which the individual 'refers,' consciously or unconsciously in the shaping of his/her attitudes and beliefs and values on a given subject or in the formation of his/her conduct." Although each person is a member of a variety of communities at any given time, only a select few function as his/her reference group in the full sense of the term. The community that functions as one's ultimate reference group or "community of reference" is the particular community from which she gains her fundamental identity [VK 2003:255]. This community functions as the school of formation.

So how does a community of reference function as a school of formation? They way it does this is by teaching its members to learn to link both the past and the future. In this way the members of the community retain the memory of their history. This way of formation helps to generate hope. Hence Josiah Royce uses the terms a "community of memory" and "a community of hope" to denote a reference community.

History also plays a role in the formation of the members of a community. A community is formed by its history. As a process to formation the Community teaches its members to being with learning their past and extend into the future. We may call this as the "constitutive narrative" of a community. Grenz points out that this "constitutive narrative" does not view time merely as a continuous flow of qualitatively meaningless sensations. Rather, in telling its story, a community punctuates the present—the day, the week, the season, the year—with a sense of the transcendent and thereby presents time as a meaningful whole [VK 2003:255]. This is what Grenz writes in his essay *Ecclesiology*,

> "The constitutive narrative begins "in the beginning," with the primal event that called the community into being, and it includes the crucial milestones that mark its subsequent trajectory. More important than merely reselling past occurrences, however, reciting the constitutive past narrative places the contemporary community within the primal events that constituted their fore bearers as this particular community. The act of reciting reconstitutes the community in the present as the contemporary embodiment of a communal tradition the spans the years." [VK 2003:255].

The constitutive narrative is highlighted through sacred practices that anthropologists call "rites of intensification". Through these rituals the community is assembled or brought together. The consequence of which is the strengthening of group solidarity, and reinforcement of commitment to its beliefs". These "practices of commitment" define the community way of life as well as the patterns of loyalty and obligations that keep the community alive. Participation in these acts solidifies the "feelings" of community sensed by the group members [VK 2003:256].

Community practicing Social Control

Life in a community is a process of formation which regulates the behaviour of each member. As social-control on its members formation restricts their actions within the limits of the community's common values and established norms, for example, monogamy among Christians. With the exercise of social control the members voluntarily live up to a set values and norm which is expected of them. Such control brings sanctions, sanctions which are both positive and negative in nature. But the aim of such sanctions is to invigorate people to accede to norms which are set from time to time. This process in the community strengthens group-life and also fosters development of individuals, which enables them to know 'what to think' and 'what not to think', 'what to do' and 'what not to do'.

Social control is a pervasive feature in every community. It is vital for establishing for maintaining social order and to check deviant tendencies and behaviours. Social control mechanisms are viewed as those arrangement which does two things: firstly, it prevents such tendencies in individuals; and secondly it prevents the tendencies to take a full-fledged deviant form [BHC 1965:65].

Community in Context of Social Changes

The scope of community in the individual's life has gradually changed. As the society has become more industrialised and impersonal, the boundaries of society have become imprecise. A consequence of industrialism has been suburbanisation, i.e. the movement of people out of the central district to the periphery of the urban sprawl, and thereby increased separation of place of work and place of residence. In new suburban areas people look for new communities to forge their sense of belonging. Elaborate sociological investigations were focused on community-life which revealed the reality of its power. Moreover this power was derived from multiple sources which function as the hub of politics [EB-20 1973:790]. Thus a community collaborates with other groups of people in geographic proximity, special interest, or similar situations to address issues affecting their well-being.

All this was true in the industrial and modern stage of the first half of the twentieth century. Social changes occurred with the onset of the revolutionary age of space and communication. With digital access to historical data, narratives, and personalities; and quick visibility of the past culture, artefacts, monuments and events, the age of post-modernity manifested itself. People could easily pick and choose, cut and paste, and blend whatever they liked from history. This accessibility has now become a global reality leading to a blended culture of various historical periods particularly in art and architecture. Thanks to the digital devices. Due to this privilege of using the past material in new ways, the relevance of history as a progressive and exploratory exercise is viewed to have reached its end.

Whatever might be the view of the postmodernists, the communal history does not end in the past, but extends into the future. As a result, a community turns the gaze of its members toward the future, anticipating the continuation of, and even the further development of the community. Not only does the community sense that it is moving towards an ideal that lies before it, more importantly, it expectantly looks to the ideal or "eschatological" future, when the purpose and goals—the *telos*—of the community will be fully actualised. This expectation of a glorious future serves as an ongoing admonition to lift its members to embody the communal vision in the present.

* * * *

Social Change Must Precede Political Change

But communities don't flourish automatically until two things are done. First that the hurdles against flourishing are to be identified and eliminated; and second that the social conditions are made conducive for people to flourish. It was for this reason that Dr Ambedkar maintained a difference of opinion with Mahatma Gandhi. Unlike the Mahatma he held that to make democracy to flourish properly social change must pave the way for political change. Social change should come before political change.

While Mahatma Gandhi initiated movements for political emancipation from the British in three phases beginning from 1920, namely, Non-Cooperation, Civil Disobedience and Quit India, Dr Ambedkar led movements for social reform and equal rights for the Untouchables. Towards this end he led 5000 Dalits in March 1927 to taste water from the public *chawder* tank in Mahad as per the municipal ruling that 'Mahad tank was open to all irrespective of their caste'. He publicly burned *Manusmriti* on the Christmas Day of 1927, and led *Satyagraha* on 2nd March 1930 with B.K. Gaikwad for entry of Untouchables into the prestigious *Kalaram* Temple in Nasik [DM 2019:184].

Dr Ambedkar was clear that without the removal of caste discrimination there could be no flourishing of people. In this line of thinking he wrote,

> "A democratic form of government presupposes a democratic form of society. The formal framework of democracy is of no value and would indeed be a misfit if there was no social democracy. The politicians never realized that democracy was not a form of government. It was essentially a form of society. It may not be necessary for a democratic society to be marked by unity, by community of purpose, by loyalty to public ends and by mutuality of sympathy. But it does unmistakably involve two things. The first is an attitude of mind, an attitude of respect and equality towards their fellows. The second is a social organization free from rigid social barriers. Democracy is incompatible and inconsistent with isolation and exclusiveness, resulting in the distinction between the privileged and the unprivileged." [BAWS Vol-1 1989:222]

From the above excerpt taken from Dr Ambedkar's public address titled *Ranade, Gandhi and Jinnah* in 1943 which he had delivered on the occasion of Mahadeo Govind Ranade's 101st birth celebration, he warned that mere political democracy, without democratization of society, would not allow democracy to put down deeper roots in the India. In this line of reasoning it must be admitted that democracy is very unlike the feudal society which brought benefits to the aristocratic families alone. Moreover democracy being an associated way of life aims to facilitate development and flourishing of all people. Communist may also do so but unlike democracy there is neither freedom nor participation nor engagement of the masses in the political life of the country under their rule.

Cisco Caste Discrimination Case

In India the social barrier to make the masses to flourish is neither feudalism nor communism nor capitalism; the culprit is the caste system and Brahmanism's patriarchy to which, alas, even the victim readily submits. Casteist discrimination has now taken global proportion. A latest report of a case from the United States of America is a typical example of it. The case was covered by Anupama Rao of Barnard College, Columbia University NY and published on the portal of *Scroll.in* website article *Cisco Caste Discrimination Case* (visited on 12.07.2020). She reported that,

> "The Cisco case bears the burden of making anti-Dalit prejudice legible to American civil rights law as an extreme form of social disability attached to those formerly classified as "Untouchable". … This case busts the myth of South Asian diaspora as a monolithic community and a model minority, the 'other one percent'. The case makes caste internationally visible as the practice of social exclusion that is materially consequential."

The story is this. The California regulators filed a suit in the federal court on June 30th 2020 against Cisco Systems Inc., alleging that the company failed to prevent discrimination, harassment and retaliation against a Dalit engineer, anonymised as "John Doe" in the filing. The complaint, *Department of Fair Employment and Housing*, described a hostile work environment that resulted in "John Doe" receiving less pay, fewer opportunities for advancement and otherwise suffering inferior terms and conditions of employment. The suit named Cisco and its two employees Sundar Iyer and Ramana Kompella, who served in a supervisory capacity over John Doe at varying times. It was reported that

> "There were eight charges with multiple counts against them. These were "Retaliation", "Failure to take all reasonable steps to prevent discrimination, harassment, and retaliation", and "Discrimination on the Basis of Religion, Ancestry, National Origin/Ethnicity and Race/Colour."

This is as far as legal provisions for civil protection in the United States is concerned. In the Indian Constitution dalits, who are termed as Scheduled Castes, are given a unique form of civil right law called *reservations*. It describes the condition of the people of Scheduled Castes (SC) and Scheduled Tribes (ST) origin as an enduring group of disadvantaged people suffering from social and economic *backwardness* due to Caste System. Unlike the legal provisions in Civil Rights Act 1964 in the United States which aims at *equality of opportunity* for the African-American, the reservation in the Indian Constitution aims at *equality of outcome*. Thanks to Dr Ambedkar that the inclusion of Article-17 in the Indian Constitution abolished untouchability and prescribed a system of compensatory discrimination for its victims and their descendants, including an unusual and robust set of criminal law provisions, for instance, the Prevention of Atrocities Act, that were instituted to protect these communities from violence by the dominant, so called the upper-castes.

It must be admitted that the US Courts are inexperienced to deal with cases connected with casteist incidences, which are of different nature from raciest incidences of discrimination and atrocities. As far as India is concerned the constitutional commitment to social and economic advancement of SC and ST have guided the Courts to pass decrees. In fact the Indian Courts' preferential treatment of SC and ST not only springs from constitutional commitment, but it is considered as remedial measure for social inequality.

Beside the above opinion, Anupama Rao makes another straight observation drawing a line under disfavor that is being done to the disadvantaged communities. This is what she writes,

"Ironically, affirmative action policies that are remedial in their conception are now criticized, whether in India or the United States, for introducing exception and inequality in the domain of liberal equality. It is true that there is a very wide gap between progressive legislation and equitable outcome in case law. However, this is not the reason why the state is actively rolling back civil rights legislation, both in India and in the United States. In the process and as a consequence, those who suffer the disability of caste or race are now viewed as the undeserving beneficiaries of affirmative action policy, while the true beneficiaries of inherited privilege redefine their privilege as "merit".

Granted that the Cisco Caste Discrimination case in the US has been recommended as an essential reading for Human Rights department to alert them that 'there could be minorities within minorities, and that Indians are far from being a uniform or homogeneous group'; for Dalits in India it is a dismal piece of news. It means that the caste system has now taken global proportion among the Indian diaspora communities. This disease of mind has now spread world over and taken roots outside its locus of origin.

This also shows that the flourishing of Dalits within the Indian diaspora community has been restricted. As is the case of "John Doe" in the US, so are similar cases in other foreign lands; to wit a Dalit can be twice oppressed—first as an *immigrant* in that country; and second as an *Untouchable* by the diaspora. A way out for Dalits to emancipate themselves from this fix is to organize themslves as communities to resist casteist and resist tyranny. It is, therefore, important that as students of the Bible we must seek the foundation and principles of *Flourishing Communities* within the tradition of our own scriptures. This is also important from a sociological point of view, because life and work of Lord Jesus Christ—his incarnation, passion, crucifixion, resurrection, ascension and return—as set out in the scripture is the *constitutive narrative* of the Christian community. This Christ-event or the *exodus of Christ* is affirmed in our liturgy,

"Christ has died, Christ is risen, Christ shall come again."

Therefore, the foundation and principles for everything else which is derived socially or deduced intellectually must fit in this frame of Christ event. This is for two reasons.

Firstly, it gives confidence to the believing sisters and brothers in partnership with the gospel; and *secondly*, it reinforces our own commitment to mission in partnership with God. Moreover, for those who accept the authority of scripture, they derive their inspiration, directions, corrections and ideals from it. For this reason our foundation and principles of *Flourishing Communities* set within its biblical frame of reference will not only shape our theoretical understanding correctly, but also shape our personal lives to be like Jesus so that we may rightly work to enable others to flourish. Then with this in place—i.e. our theory and lifestyle—we ourselves will have both intellectual and interior resources to combat casteism.

We, however, cannot end our study at this point without discussing the analysis of Dr Ambedkar on this subject. Sometime after the First World War in 1918 Dr Ambedkar wrote a critical review on Bertrand Russell's *Principles of Social Reconstruction* in the "Journal of Indian Economic Society" [BAWS Vol-1 1989:483]. Though the formal discourse on *Flourishing Communities* had not developed then, Russell, nevertheless, addressed the wreckages of the Great War by seeking some way to help the devastated communities to flourish again. In his article on social reconstruction Russell had propounded pacifism by changing one's *impulses* as a prevention of war. Citing thinkers like Angell who in his *Great Illusion* attempted to show that "in the calculus of war loss prevails over gain", Ambedkar showed that Russell's antidote to war was based on an entirely different approach i.e. human *impulse*. Russell believes, writes Dr Ambedkar,

> "It is not by reason alone that wars can be prevented but by positive life of impulses and passions antagonistic to those that lead to war. It is the life of impulse that needs to be changed, not only the life of conscious thought."

Dr Ambedkar on the one hand greatly appreciates Russell's insights connecting psychology to sociology, on the other applying his own line of reasoning he critiques him. But he did this in order to help the readers not to misunderstand Russell.

Using Ambedkar's Insights for Flourishing Communities

What is true of restructuring society, is applicable for making communities to flourish. Our interest here, however, is not in Bertrand Russell, but in Dr Ambedkar's views. In reviewing Russell he used three insights, namely, Impulse and Institution; Creative Impulse and Possessive Impulse; Pain Economy and Pleasure Economy. Let us unpack the ideas of these insights under four headings in the sections below.

1. Promote Circumstances to Modify Impulses beneficial to flourish

In the early twentieth century science of psychology was coming up with new perspectives. One such perspective was about the source that moves a human being to *act*. The idea that the springs of human action were stimulated by external circumstances was abandoned. The criticism was that instead of recognizing his pro-active state, it had reduced human beings to a dormant state. Dr Ambedkar pointed out that according to behavioristic psychology, human being was born with interior tendencies to act. External circumstances did not induce activity; instead it only redirected it. These *tendencies to act* became modified by the circumstances in the social environment in which they operated. The modifications in the original tendencies were regarded as of highest importance. They constituted education in the widest sense of the word.

All modifications, however, were not equally valuable and it was the business of the reformer to deal with the *circumstances* of these modifications. They must eliminate the *circumstances* that modify tendencies that are socially adverse; and promote those that modify them for the social betterment. Elimination and preservation also involve *institutions*. Dr Ambedkar in line with Russell accepted that social institutions were constituted by human beings and along with them they also are being constantly modified for better or for worse. The most important thing here was not dealings with the circumstances of modification as such, but the possibility of *infinite* of modifications.

This *infiniteness* of possibilities was to be viewed as the gateway to study the various perspectives thereby judging the benefits or the harms that is done by political and social institutions. Herein lies the insight for making a community flourish. That is to say the courage and wisdom to *eliminate the circumstances* in the social environment that modify human impulse and institutions for the worse and conversely to *promote circumstances* that modify them to be beneficial.

2. *Allow Impulses to Trigger Activities for Flourishing*

According to Dr Ambedkar human impulses must not be inhibited. He contends that, "Every impulse if uninhibited, will lead to some creative act." However, what is produced individually or collectively by the *impulse* can be used in different ways. As far as what is produced collectively "no one can set up a right of appropriation to anything that is produced by common efforts nor to anything that is of joint use." Granted that production originates in impulse, but the use or appropriation of the product can be distinctly personal or communal. A good example for this is a family. This is what he writes to illustrate a product and its appropriation:

> "No member, it can be said without fear of being challenged, will ever set up a right of private appropriation of the articles of the Table or to the articles of decoration just as nobody will set up a right of exclusive ownership regarding public monuments. They are *of the house*. But every one of the family will surely set up a right to the exclusive use of his or her clothes. They are *of the individual*." [BAWS Vol.1 1989:492]

It is clear that for making a community to flourish, the *impulse* of its individual members must be given scope, so that with this power of creativity they produce proper things to meet the needs of individuals and community. It must be highlighted that to be creative is to be active, and that activity leads to growth, not quietism.

3. *Utility of Money to Sustain Activities to Flourish*

Dr Ambedkar critiqued the misconception that hovered over Russell's biblical phrase "love of money". Dr Ambedkar critiqued Russell's deductions that,

> "This love of money leads people to mutilate their own nature from a mistaken theory of what constitutes success and to give admiration to enterprises which add nothing to human welfare. It promotes a dead uniformity of character and purpose, a diminution in the joy of life, and a stress and strain which leaves whole communities weary, discouraged and disillusioned." [BAWS Vol.1 1989:488].

Dr Ambedkar does not agree with Russell on this point. In Dr Ambedkar's line of reasoning, without economic activity there could be no flourishing of human communities. By discussing the economies of pain and pleasure he shows that money in itself was nothing but an instrument of utility to achieve certain ends. But the phrase "love of money", as Dr Ambedkar showed, was a phrase with moral baggage. Dr Ambedkar was right. Bertrand had lifted this phrase directly from Saint Paul's letter to Timothy in the New Testament,

> "For *the love of money* is a root of all kinds of evil. Some people, eager for money, have wandered from the faith and pierced themselves with many grief." (1 Timothy 6.10).

Some two thousand years ago, when this text was composed, the socio-economic conditions were entirely different. In the ancient world the production from human labor was extremely low, and no efforts could augment its return. As a result of which poverty used to permeate the whole world. In that context, argued Dr Ambedkar, it was but natural that moralists should have preached appreciating poverty and renunciation of worldly desires only because it was impossible to have them. Interestingly conditions had not changed even till the twentieth century AD when global society after the Great War was reduced to live in the *pain economy.*

The belief of a society of *pain economy* is that a thing must be bad if it cannot be had. Conversely the belief of the society of *pleasure economy,* which is addicted to conspicuous consumption, is that a thing must be nasty if it was cheap. Thereon Dr Ambedkar went on to state that,

> "The misconception (about the phrase *love of money*) arises from the fact that Russell criticizes the love on money without inquiring into the purpose of it. In a healthy mind, it may be urged, there is no such thing as love of money in the abstract. Love of money is always *for something* and it is the purpose embodied in that "for something" that will endow it with credit or cover it with shame. Having regard to this, there can be no "dead uniformity of character" among the individuals, for though actuated by love of money, their purposes on different occasions are likely to be different. Thus even love of money as a pursuit may result in a variety of character." [BAWS Vol.1 1989:489].

Dr Ambedkar's leading idea in the above excerpts is not that the love of money was evil *per se*; rather the good or evil is determined by the end that is achieved by means of *it*. For a community to flourish it should use money as the *means* to achieve a proper end. Without money there cannot be any flourishing.

It must be admitted that Dr Ambedkar's insights in the above three sections connect individual to society or community. The insight for making a community to flourish depends upon the right operation of the relationship of individuals to their community.

§ § §

References

[BAWS] Writings and Speeches. *Babasaheb Dr B.R. Ambedkar*, Volume-1 (1989) Mumbai.

 [DM] Daniel. Monodeep, *Society in India: Dr Ambedkar's Vision* (2019) ISPCK. New Delhi.

[EB] *Encyclopaedia Britannica Volume* -20 (1973) William Benton Publisher. Chicago.

[JG] Jacob. Godson, *Community in the writings of Jurgen Moltmann for an Indian Ecclesiology* (2019) ISPCK New Delhi.

[VK] Vanhoozer. Kevin J. (Editor), *Cambridge Companion to Postmodern Theology* (2003) Cambridge University Press. Cambridge U.K.

Chapter 2

Hindrance to Flourishing

For our communities to flourish it is important to analyse their nature and mechanisms in the context of India. Granted that bodily existence of human beings, in line with Jurgen Moltmann's opinion, entails a social existence, the society is in itself an organized entity [JG 2019: 2]. It must at once be recognized that communities within the larger frame of society are organized on the basis of caste system. In the vernacular, the system is known as the *varna-ashram-dharma*. In this chapter we will develop our understanding of two things. Firstly concerning community; and secondly concerning caste. This will help us to identify the hindrance which restrains communities in India to flourish. Help from sociology is unavoidable for this.

Towards an Understanding of Caste System in India

Despite the ongoing social changes that have been proceeding all around, the community life in India has largely been stagnant. This is so due to the casteist nature of the communities which is deeply rooted in the Hindu religious thought. The social changes during the long stretch of Islamic rulers, or due to British colonial rule or the Industrialisation or urbanisation or due to Ambedkar's constitution in independent India, none of the social changes succeeded to shift the thinking of people as far as caste is concerned. Caste system is a way of organising society of various communities placing each within the parameter of four castes at unequal social levels.

Indologists broadly classify four caste groups, namely, *Brahmin* or the priestly caste; *Kshatriya* or the warrior caste; *Vaishya* or the trading caste; *Shudra* or the servile caste. This system is called the *varna-ashram-dharma* which is translated as station-stage-obligation [DM 2016:5]. Each caste in the system is divided further into diverse sub-castes. Then there are those who are outside the structure of the four tier caste-system, these are the socially excluded people *bahishkrit samaj* who describe themselves as *Dalit* and more recently after their conversion as Neo-Buddhists particularly in Maharashtra.

The word *Dalit* is derived from the root *Dal,* incidentally common to both Hebrew and Sanskrit. In both languages it has the same meaning i.e. crushed, weak, split-open, and trampled upon [MJ 1994:1-34]. Before we tackle the question of the social operation of caste let us briefly comprehend what caste system is. Following the cue set by Prof Romila Thapar, a well-known cultural historian, we will use two perspectives to comprehend Caste-System. These are caste and lineage. The first perspective is of European scholars; the second is the perspective of an Indian scholar. The truth can be view from both perspectives, but the thing that cannot be overlooked is the glaring fact of socio-cultural practice of exclusion, expulsion and exploitation of the masses.

Caste

Caste utilises quintessential practices segregation, customs and occupation to maintain itself. It must be admitted that when caste-system operates in society in the above three manners it becomes casteism. Let us discuss each of these three practices.

Segregation has a trait of racial separation in which Aryans constitute the so called 'upper caste'. The root of this perspective lies in the term *Varna*, which categorises society into four groups as we have seen above, namely, *Brahmin, Kshatriya, Vaishya* and *Shudra*. The root meaning of *Varna* is colour [SA 2005:11]. Max Muller further developed this racial theory and added to it the ideas of Aryan migration from the Central Asia and subjugation of the people of river Indus.

> "The concept was understood to be referring to the pigmentation of the skin. This gave credence to the late eighteenth century idea of Aryan superiority then current in Europe. The practice of endogamy was believed to have preserved the racial purity of the so-called upper castes; this however cannot be guaranteed with any certainty." [DM 2007:68].

This theory of Aryan Invasion has been contested by the right wing scholars, nonetheless, the preservation of superiority by the *Arya* or superior castes in the practice of untouchability against Dalits continues unabated.

The family customs had a strong strait of segregation. The separation in the practice of commensality in the family practically excludes the aliens. It was assumed to have worked to establish the separation of the short-stature and dark-skinned people from the fair Aryans [DM 2007:68].

The pervasive practice of fixed occupations for fixed castes also has to be reckoned with. The theory behind this practice is that various occupational tasks gave rise to guilds. These guilds eventually differentiated themselves into hierarchical castes. This was based on the notion of the Indian idyllic community. In other words each village was completely self-sufficient, where each caste community was involved in doing its own work as its occupation. Romila Thapar writes.

> "The village community was seen as the root of Indo-European life and it was thought that in the Indian village community Europe has rediscovered its origin." [TR 2000:28].

The religious justification for the caste system is based on the *Purushasukta* which is the hymn of creation in the Rig Veda. It describes a cosmic sacrifice of *Purusha* out of whose body the four Varnas were said to have sprung: the *Brahmins* out of his mouth, the *Kashtriyas* out of his arm, the *Vaishyas* out of his thighs and *Shudra* out of his feet. In this order the first three came to be regarded as superior and the Shudra was the lowest set apart to serve the three above him. No mention was made of those who were ousted from this structure of four fold-tier *varna* categories.

The people from the first three castes, therefore, assumed dominant positions. Traditionally out of them came the teachers of scripture and philosophy, the rulers, the warriors and the traders.

Lineage

Romila prefers to use lineage *Vansha* (descendants) as a tool for historical analysis of the Indian society [TR 2000:75]. She notes that not only the rise and establish emend of the four tier caste but their social status and economic privilege were also determined and justified by *vansha*. The status of the few, who after the rise of state system monopolised the system, had to be duly justified. To fulfil this need, long list of descendants or *vansha* came to be composed. The socio-historical values of such *vanshavalis* or lineages lie in the myths that control the deepest levels of our people's consciousness. Romila Thapar writes,

> "The significance of myth to the historian lies more in its being the self-image of a given culture, expressing its social assumptions." [TR 2000:125].

Romila points out that these myths of lineage have preserved the cultural pasts of the dominant caste groups in India. Those who do not find themselves in these lists are excluded from the mainstream of the society. As a result of which the first three castes became the dominant force in society. The economic reality of the *Kshatriyas* amassing most of the wealth and *Brahmins* sharing it by way of receiving large gifts gave the benefit of leadership to these so called the 'upper' caste people. As a lineage evolved into monarchy, the Brahmins continued to play their role as the legitimisers of the Kshatriya Rajas and the Rajas in turn kept reinforcing the superior status of the Brahmin priests. In this social transaction the authority, however, remained intact with the dominant castes [DM 2007:69].

In the above discussion from the two perspectives embedded in the practice of caste and lineage, it is clear the the caste system is as complex social reality is oppressive and unjust. Let us study its complexity in the section below.

Granted that the *varna-ashrama-dharma* i.e. station-stage-obligation or Caste System, has been idealised in the traditional Indian literature, the fact of the matter is that it was enforced, adopted and adapted due to various economic and political reasons. Therefore, its prevalence is evident in the striking presence of subordinated populations who are regarded as distinct and labelled as *untouchables* and *tribal.* Susan Bayly, a social anthropologist in Cambridge University UK, underscores the complex nature of this system by pointing out its various versions. She underscores three modes of existence and conduct that aggregated the reinforcement of the caste system since the nineteenth century:

> One, the way of life of the kingly warrior or the person of prowess.
>
> Two, the way of life of the service-provider i.e. both the literate priestly and the specialist record-keeper.
>
> Three, the way of life of the settled person of worth, i.e. the agriculturist and the businessman who favoured the ascetic renounced than the Brahmin priest.

Bayly argues that although till the nineteenth century these three modes, namely, the person of prowess, the service provider and thereby the settled person of worth, lived in uneasy synthesis, a very large populace lived and conducted themselves in a very uncastelike manner. However, the casteist practices were aggravated with the expansion of the British interest by imposing taxes in agrarian sectors, expansion of civil administration, establishment of army, founding of mills and construction of infrastructure and extension of railways. In all these sectors, labour was needed in unskilled work and removing waste for which the pollution-removers were identified and employed. These castes crystallised in a legal way particularly with the exercise of census where people were identified, named and classified as castes [DM 2016:5].

Nevertheless, the British were not the sole contributors to this phenomenon; they merely took advantage of the trait that easily was available in culture. Let us take just one case as an example. East India Company had decided to remove the Brahmin rulers from the former Martha realms. There was a threat that this decision might be challenged. However, East India Company used the caste logic to reinforce their decision. James Grant Duff, Company's chronicler, argued that 'the Peshwas were not and never had been rightful rulers; they were Brahmins whose proper sphere in life was that of priest and scribe. So it could only have been through guile and subversion that their line had achieved power at the expense of the descendants of Shivaji Bhonsle [DM 2016:6].

Under the East India Company expansionist policies of the nineteenth century, different versions of caste system developed. Consequently uncastelike populace were either absorbed in a caste or excluded as untouchables. In Bayly's research—*Caste, Society and Politics in India (1999)*—we can identify three, namely, the Brahmin, the Kshatriya and the Vaishya versions respectively. One common feature all versions shared was to subordinate Dalits under the priestly Brahmin and the thread-wearing warrior dynasty to work as pollution-removers with no enjoyment of human rights as such.

The *Brahmins*, as service providers, had a well-known version of caste where social segregation was ordered to the advantage of the priestly castes in a descending order of purity. According to this various groups or communities were placed into four levels of descending order of purity. *Brahmin* caste was placed on top. From among the diverse groups of Brahmins various kinds of priests were prepared, some to teach, others to cremate the dead, still others to do the rituals *karmakanda*. At the second level was *Kshatriya* caste. These were the warriors. At the third level was the *Vaishya* caste. These are business communities, for instance, the bania community. At the fourth level was the *Shudra* caste. These were the servile people who were made to serve those above them. The rest were the untouchable *Dalits* unfit for associating with the three top clean castes Suvarnas.

The Kshatriya, as men of prowess, also had a version of caste for themselves. If purity was the anxiety of the Brahmans, legitimacy was for Kshatriya. Both had to do with possession social and political power. The Kshatriya version was for legitimising themselves as rulers and defenders. This was acutely felt by Shivaji Bhonsle (1630-80) who needed to be rescued from his rustic non-*Dwija* (i.e. non twice-born) origin and accommodated in a caste which would legitimise him as a Maratha ruler. This was done by Brahmins who were linked with Varanasi and Mewar. They performed the ceremony of investiture of Shivaji with the sacred thread, anointing his body with sweet and transforming essences of Brahminical rituals particularly milk, curd and ghee which were all nurturing gifts of the holy cow. However, the accommodation of non-*Dwija* as *Kshatriya* did not end with legitimising kingship. Groups that wanted to be recruited as soldiers were willing to follow their patrons who willingly vested them a *jati* title and other casteist designations. Caste formations in recent past centuries bear the titles *Jat, Koli* and *Kambli*. Re-engaging them into arms-bearing groups over a period of time they started to behave like a caste except that they did not worry about attaching significance to the Brahmins or standards of purity [DM 2016:7].

The settled people of worth associated themselves as the third caste, i.e. *Vaishya*, developed their own version of caste system. These communities were variously known as *bania* or *mahajan* or *saukar*. During the depression of 1830s and with the eclipse of Mughals and incoming of East India Company, many emerged as traders and specialists in handling money.

Some consolidated their hold on State and military finance while others became revenue collectors and money-lenders. Many increased their fortunes by grabbing the land rights from the original land owners.

Whatever may be the case they became wealthy by exploiting fiscal opportunities but to be credit-worthy they needed respectability. The injunction of the Shastra placed the handlers of money and goods slightly above the *Shudras*, which was still far below in the social scale. The way to alleviate was to adopt a new way of life, namely, of dharmic correctness. The aim for the *Vaishyas* was to gain respectability by distancing themselves from the *Shudras* and their getting status closer to the *Brahmin-Kshatriya*. With this in view the *Vaishya*-traders did their best to become impeccable observers of *dharmic* injunction of purity.

> "The evil would have been lesser had the caste system been merely confined to distinguish the so called the ritually clean from the polluted castes. What compounds the problem is that definite occupations have been fixed with particular castes. The idea is that one must do what one was born for i.e. unclean tasks for unclean castes, and clean tasks for clean castes. This is so because caste and occupation are fixed by birth. So a *shudra* cannot undertake a priestly profession and vice-versa down the line of descending purity.
>
> Similarly marriage is also controlled by endogamous practices of castes, but exogamous across the *gotra* of a caste. To preserve the caste system by observing the occupation, marriage and food regulations, and respecting the restriction of social intercourse regarded as *dharma*.
>
> Economy is also regulated along the caste lines, the Dalits suffer the misery of poverty and degradation due to graded inequality, fixity of occupation and fixation of people which are three basic traits of the caste system according to Dr Ambedkar." [DM 2016:8].

The drawback of this system is this, that a very large population has been left out of being included in a caste. These communities are perceived as carriers of pollution. They, therefore, are Untouchables, who prefer to describe themselves as Dalits or Neo-Buddhists. It is interesting to note that over a period of time Scheduled Castes also have developed their own version of Caste System. Their different communities have placed themselves above one another in a caste-like manner.

Caste system is the blight of the very fibre and every aspect of a free and equal society. As a result of which despite our political independence, we have not yet been emancipated from caste-slavery in our society. The fruition of the divine blessing promised to Abraham (Genesis 22.16-18) and the vision of Mahatma Jotirao Phule and Dr Ambedkar will truly come to pass only with complete annihilation of caste [DM 2016:9].

Patriarchy of Casteist Colour

The other hindrance for communities to flourish which is interlaced with caste system is patriarchy. This aspect has not been brought up in the earlier chapter, therefore, it is necessary that we study it at this point. In the patriarchal system, the males are cared for and are privileged more than the female members. This is not only true of family, but also of the community and society. However, the brahminical patriarchy has a distinct flavour.

Granted that patriarchy places women under men in status and prestige, but they are also placed under and above one another according to their caste. This makes the graded inequality of caste system more complex. It means that a Brahmin women are inferior to Brahmin men but are superior to Kshatriya men. Down the line of caste descent the untouchable men also have a group, namely their women, to tyrannize and exploit [RAS 2020:64]. The result of this arrangement is severe. Rathore writes,

"This is Brahminical patriarchy, where all castes and genders are ranked and kept in place by having the burden of their inequalities compensated by the benefit of exploiting their subordinates. Untouchable women, at the bottom of the bottom, then are the only ones who get no solace in the system. But as the most vulnerable they are least in a position to topple it." [RAS 2020:64].

The casteist patriarchy is peculiar. It is clear that Brahmin males benefit most from it, but everyone else also find a place in it and so they do their part to maintain the status quo. Rathore notes that brahmanical patriarchy does not refer to the patriarchal practices followed by Brahmins; instead, it represents the graded nature of patriarchy in India. It is just like those who regardless of their gender, age or caste followed Brahmanism which is another name for caste system. When a person believes, practices, preaches or encourages any kind of discrimination based on casteist hierarchical structure of graded inequality that person follows Brahmanism or caste system [RAS 2020:64].

Exploring Connection of Caste with Community

The idea that castes operate like a wider community each constituted of several *gotra* is too simplistic. Similarly, Marxist understanding of social classes, like the bourgeoisie and proletariat, operating on principles of organised but antagonistic communities is also inapplicable for a caste structured society. As far as castes are concerned, they are organised in graded inequality of social hierarchy and ranking, but the inter-caste relationship is complicated. According to Rathore, this complication is due to the weird relationship of emotional antagonism and practical cooperation between castes which comes into play simultaneously. Despite the feeling of revulsion and disgust against the Scheduled Castes, toleration is exercised and encouragement is offered to them to clean up the streets [RAS 2020:63]. Rathore explains this as below,

> "Simple inequality, such as that of Marxist class antagonism, generates discontent that may easily sow the seeds of revolution. Graded inequality, on the contrary, invites all people in a society to celebrate inequality and share in its spoils. It thus makes revolution rare, while also accounting for the long stability of orthodoxy and inequality throughout the long history of India—a history where Marxist revolution makes little sense, as it concerns class and not caste. Under the stable and profoundly inegalitarian castes of graded inequality, every caste has another community that it may freely and legally exploit, even as it suffers from exploitation. Only the untouchables, those outside of the *varna* system that gave birth to the caste system, have no group below them." [RAS 2020:64].

Each Caste is a wider community constituted of various *gotras* or 'little communities'. Despite exploitation of a caste by the one above them, all castes get some advantage from the exploits of the system. So all are happily settled in their own little corner and cooperate only to the extent the caste-duty demands from them. Communities and Castes, both are strongly connected with each other. Communities are unequally ranked in casteist society—dominant versus subservient—depending on the status of their castes. This graded inequality resulting in segregation and untouchability is the unique characteristic of communities in India.

§ § §

References

[BHC] Brearley. H. C. 1965. "*The Nature of Social Control*", In Joseph S. Rock st. Al. (Ed) *Social Control*, Affliated East West Press: New Delhi.

[DM] Daniel. Monodeep, 2016. *From People to Community*. New Delhi. ISPCK.

[DM] Daniel. Monodeep, 2007. *Models of Leadership in the Indian Church: An Evaluation*, published in Studies in World Christianity Vol-13 Part-1. Edinburgh.

[EB] *Encyclopaedia Britannica* Volume1973) 20-) William Benton Publisher. Chicago.

[JG] Jacob. Godson, *Community in the Writings of Jürgen Moltmann for an Indian Ecclesiology* (2019) ISPCK New Delhi.

[MJ] Massey. James, 1994. *Towards Dalit Hermeneutics: Rereading the Text, the History and the Literature.* New Delhi. ISPCK.

[SA] Sen. Amartya, 2005. *The Argumentative Indian: Writings on Indian History, Culture and Identity.* London. Penguin Books.

[RAS] Rathore. Aakash Singh, *Ambedkar Preamble: A Secret History of the Constitution of India* (2020) Vintage Penguin Books. Gurugram.

[TR] Thapar. Romila, 2000. *Cultural Pasts: Essays in Early Indian History.* New Delhi. Oxford University Press.

[VK] Vanhoozer. Kevin J. (Editor), *Cambridge Companion to Postmodern Theology* (2003) Cambridge University Press. Cambridge U.K.

Chapter 3

Foundations for Flourishing: Justice and Reconciled Diversity

We are human. The basic nature of human beings is that we live in communities. This is due to the fact that none of us can be completely independent, we are dependent on others to meet our needs. The human life in a community ensures that the needs of all individuals are met. The text from the New Testament is one example to show this interdependence of human beings to help each other to survive through difficult times. The record of how able people were selected to help the widows of the neonate Christian community is in the Acts of the Apostles. This is what is recorded in the text,

"In those days when the number of disciples was increasing, the Hellenistic Jews among them complained against the Hebraic Jews because their widows were being overlooked in the daily distribution of food. So the Twelve gathered all the disciples together and said, "It would not be right for us to neglect the ministry of the word of God in order to wait on tables. Brothers and sisters, choose seven men from among you who are known to be full of the Spirit and wisdom. We will turn this responsibility over to them and will give our attention to prayer and the ministry of the word. This proposal pleased the whole group. They chose Stephen, a man full of faith and of the Holy Spirit; also Philip, Procorus, Nicanor, Timon, Pamenas, and Nicolas from Antioch, convert to Judaism. They presented these men to the apostles, who prayed and laid their hands on them. So the word of God spread. The number of disciples in Jerusalem increased rapidly, and a large number of priests became obedient to faith." (Acts 6:1-7).

It is clear from the above text that the apostles organized a group of social workers, that is to say Deacons to attend to the needs of the widows in the neonate community in Jerusalem. The aim was not only that the meals be served to all the widows but that the distribution should be fair.

What we have read is a record of the antiquity. Interestingly, the human reality in many respects in the twenty-first century is similar. Human beings have multiple and complex needs which involve their emotions, sustenance, family, education and so on. To meet these needs human beings engage in collective effort, as no individual is sufficient and has to depend on others to meet his/her need. This is to say that interdependence of human beings is a reality. This results in the formation of well-organized communities where people can easily approach one another to meet their needs.

However, there is a downside to human life. It is their fallen nature. Here greed and selfishness comes into play causing corruption and injustice. The worst manifestation of fallen nature is social *inequality* in the human communities. These inequalities are chiefly of social and economic status. In the medieval times aristocracy and landowning feudal lords were superior to the peasants, whereas in the industrial society the workers were inferior to the capitalist who owned the means of production. In every age society has remained socially and economically unequal. There are other forms of inequalities also but to study them is beyond our scope. The point that must be underscored here is that if in the west social inequality is in the form of economic classes, then in the east it is in form of caste system. By east I specifically mean the Indian sub-continent where the word for caste-system is the *varna-ashrama dharma*, where *dharma* is akin to the law of nature. The belief is that a law cannot be violated without repercussions.

Lessons from the History of God's People

From what we have discussed above it must be admitted that communities may not always be organized or be governed for the proper benefit of all people. We know how ruling elites or aristocrats could oppress the masses. Similarly government can extort tax of exorbitant rate. We know how in the history of wars people of defeated nations were reduced to slavery or deported to captivity. Israelites also experienced this unpleasant episode in their history when they were conquered by Sennacherib in 722 BCE and Nebuchadnezzar 586 BCE. Both these rulers were ruthless and relocated a significant Israelite population in Babylon. In the process ten northern Israelite tribes were lost in the oblivion of history. Later those in Babylonian captivity survived long enough to return back to Judea. This deportation is famously referred to as the Jewish 'Exile'.

In exile the Israelites lived as subservient community to the Assyrians and later to the Babylonians. In his short poetic *Lamentations* Jeremiah writes that the community of Israelites in Babylon could not flourish.

> "After affliction and harsh labor,
> Judah has gone into exile,
> She dwells among the nations;
> She finds no resting place"

It is clear that the Israelites who were exiled to Babylon and those that were left behind in Judea to till the land were languishing. Flourishing was a far cry for them. They were humiliated of their national pride, violated of their human dignity, deprived from the worship in their Temple and their freedom to rule themselves under Torah. They were in disarray.

The conquest of Babylon by Cyrus from Persia (Isaiah 45) brought relief to the exiles and many Jews taking advantage of the lenient policies of Cyrus returned to their homeland. In the phase that followed Jewish history, life in Palestine did not prove to be easy. Nehemiah records the opposition he faced in his attempt to rebuild the walls of Jerusalem. Subsequently they were colonized by Greek, who ruthlessly implemented their policy to Hellenize the Jewish culture particularly under Antiochus Epiphanies IV. The blood bath which followed the wake of the desecration of the Temple in Jerusalem and the Maccabean revolt is recorded in the two books of Maccabees. Then came the Roman conquest. The Romans, unlike the Greeks, had a tolerant policy towards the religion and culture of the colonized people. Their interest, however, was not cultural; rather it was economic gain and political power.

Palestine during the time of the Lord Jesus was a colony of Rome. The territory was under the administration of Pontius Pilate a roman governor who represented Caesar, and Herod a puppet king. The government imposed heavy taxes and life was hard for common people. To this was the extra burden of Jewish religion which in addition to the Roman law demanded that the injunctions of the Law of Moses were also to be observed. These were quite elaborate with regard to religious observations of untouchability, the Temple tax and cult.

Given this background let us examine the attempt by the Apostles of the Lord Jesus in the New Testament times to forge a flourishing community. Did they succeed in their endeavor?

After the Example of the Apostles

The text for our consideration is taken from the Acts of the Apostles Chapter Six. The neonate community of Christians attempted to forge a common life where the needs of all people would be met and they could flourish. What we gather from Luke's record in the Acts is that the formation of the neonate community was a great experiment in social engineering. In the context of extortionist governments and ruthless rulers when social welfare as government's responsibility was not even conceived, the idea of making common people flourish began to take root in the neonate community. The issues was social in nature, that is to say, "How could people of different language groups help one another to flourish?" The answer did not lie in expecting charity from the rich although several well-to-do people helped them when the need arose (Acts 4.36-37). The way to do it was by organizing themselves into a self-governing, self-sustaining and self-propagating community. The neonate community of believers despite diversity in their language, region and ethnicity were organized around the holy apostles who 'educated' them in the life and ideals of their master Jesus Christ. They learnt together and ate together evolving into a cohesive, inspired, independent, enthusiastic and confident community. There were to be no poor among them. St Luke records how these earliest disciples had organized themselves,

> "They devoted themselves to the apostles' teaching and to fellowship, to the breaking of bread and to prayer. Everyone was filled with awe at the many wonders and signs performed by the apostles. All the believers were together and had everything in common. They sold property and possessions to give to anyone who had need.

Every day they continued to meet together in the temple courts. They broke bread in their homes and ate together with glad and sincere hearts, praising God and enjoying the favor of all the people. And the Lord added to their number daily those who were being saved." (Acts 2.42-47).

The ideal of the neonate community was to share and care for each other. Despite the social and lingual distinctiveness, they reconciled their diversities, and implemented justice within their new social environment as sharing material things with one another. In their context the nature of justice was distributive i.e. sharing and caring in home-fellowship. It was directly inspired by Jesus Christ their Lord and teacher. About Him Saint Peter spoke telling Cornelius,

"God anointed Jesus of Nazareth with the Holy Spirit and power, and how he went around *doing good* and healing all who were under the power of the devil, because God was with him," (Acts 10.38).

Hence "doing good" was not only confined among the members of the neonate community or their widows; instead the apostles set example to "do good to all" who were in need. The event of Saint Peter healing the lame beggar demonstrates this. This is what is recorded in Acts,

"One day Peter and John were going to the temple at the time of prayer—at three in the afternoon. Now a man who was lame from birth was being carried to the temple gate called Beautiful where he was put every day to beg from those going into the temple courts. When he saw Peter and John about to enter, he asked them for money. Peter looked straight at him, as did John. The Peter said, "Look at us!" So he gave them his attention, expecting to get something from them. Then Peter said, "Silver or gold I do not have, but what I do have I give you. In the name of Jesus Christ of Nazareth, walk." Taking him by the right hand, he helped him up, and instantly that man's feet and ankles became strong. He jumped to his feet and began to walk. Then he went with them into the temple courts, walking and jumping, and praising God." (Acts 3.1-8).

Primarily the episode was not about a miracle, but it was about making people independent and capable in order to be productive and worshipful members of the community. It was what we may know of as restorative justice. In other words the neonate community was not a parochial entity or a club or some trade-union which took interest only in its own members; rather its ideal was to be a blessing to all people. It was to take equal interest to make other needy or dependent people of the larger society independent and productive citizens.

Community which Cares and Shares

Let us bring our attention back to the neonate community in Jerusalem. They were a sharing and caring community, it is to say that, they practiced *distributive* and *restorative justice* within their context. It is evident from the record that the widows had to be fed from a common kitchen. Although this community was new and socially heterogeneous, they sincerely aimed to help all their needy members to flourish.

It is an accepted fact that a community is a unit of society and its members have several things in common, such as norms, ethnicity, values, identity or religion. Like any other community this neonate community also shared a common faith i.e. faith in God, the one who has revealed himself in the Bible, and in his Son Jesus Christ. They participated in the worship of the Temple in Jerusalem. This community had two distinct social strands i.e., Hebrew and Hellenic believers. They were fused in social unity and emotional oneness of soul and spirit in the new Christian community. They had been witnessing signs and wonders by the apostles e.g. healing of the lame person in Solomon's Portico in the Temple (Acts 5:12). The community believed in the commonwealth rather than in private ownership of property. It had a great concern for the poor. Wealthy people, like Barnabas, donated generously for this community. This little neonate community of believers in Jesus practiced distributive justice in their context. This is what we read as recorded by St. Luke in Acts,

> "All believers were one in heart and mind. No one claimed that any of their possessions was their own, but they shared everything they had. With great power the apostles continued to testify to the resurrection of the Lord Jesus. And God's grace was so powerfully at work in them all that there were no needy persons among them. For from time to time those who owned land or houses sold them, brought the money from the sales and put it at the apostles' feet. And it was distributed to anyone who had need.
>
> Joseph, a Levite from Cyprus, whom the apostles called Barnabas (which means "son of encouragement"), sold a field he owned and brought the money and put it at the apostles' feet." (Acts 4.32-37).

It is clear from the above excerpt that the practice of caring and sharing was the hallmark of the neonate community. These were acts of *distributive* justice. A close reading of the events in the Acts shows that the need to care and share arose due to the growth in the numbers of new believers who kept joining the neonate community. This is evident from the expression "the disciples were increasing in number". As a result of this growth new social problems began to emerge. The major problem that soon emerged was social in nature. Several people, particularly the widows, became directly dependent on the community to have their needs met. Perhaps they were those who had sold off their properties to help the needy believers, and later found it hard to meet their ends after being widowed.

Fall from the Ideals of Justice

However, human communities are never perfect. This neonate community of believers also fell prey to the cultural prejudices of their times. For example discrimination crept in through the fissures caused by distinct origin and ethnicity of various people in that new community. That the Greek widows were "overlooked in the daily distribution of food" (Acts 6.1b) was thoroughly unjust. The primitive distinction of Hebrews from the Hellenists had once again raised its ugly head. The daily distribution of ration was in the hands of the Hebrew men whose partiality was proving to be a peril to the cohesive character of the neonate community. It could be that the distribution of bread started with the Jewish women to pamper their scruples of purity. If this was so then this in itself was unacceptable to the ideal of the Christian community. It could be that bread was served first to the Hebrew widows and the bread basket which came to the Hellenic widows later contained less quantity, consequently the Hellenic widows had much less to eat.

The text also suggests that the widows did not complain rather they silently suffered this discrimination as dependent and powerless section of the community. This strongly resonates with the casteist culture which imposes silence on Dalits and more so on their women. The problem which was troubling the neonate community was placed before the apostles. It was an issue of grave injustice meted out to the Hellenic widows. They were not served their just portion of meals. As elders and founders of the community they had to promptly take a decision on grievance before it grew out of proportion affecting the reconciled-diversity of the neonate community. Granted that the measures which the apostles took saved the neonate community from premature extinction from division, yet the rightness of the measure that the apostles took is debatable.

It is important to note that Apostle did not indulge directly instead they selected seven men who were inspired in faith and were firm in character. With the common consent of people the apostles delegated to them the responsibility to organize the distribution of food. Attention should be drawn to the process of common consent i.e. the involvement of the whole community in decision making process. This should be regarded as a mark of a flourishing community. As far as their priority was concerned, the apostles clearly opted for educating the community. In other words developing "problem solving capability" as a collective exercise is also a mark of a flourishing community.

The other important thing to note is that Apostles recognized their limitations. They, therefore, did not undertake to do everything by themselves. They let the community identify leaders for themselves in whom they could place their confidence and trust. This participatory approach was a mark of democratic principle in the neonate community which is important for flourishing.

In a cultural milieu where the Jewish community had excluded the uncircumcised and the Greco-Roman societies were unequally differentiated into classes of aristocrats and plebeians, the neonate Christians aimed to forge a community which was both inclusive of all people i.e. circumcised and uncircumcised and the third gender (Acts 8.38). The community was also egalitarian i.e. both the free citizens and bonded slaves, were treated as equals. As we know, equality is an aspect of justice.

The Dilemma of the Apostles

The dilemma here was this: On the one hand if the apostles were to directly intervene they could be accused of ethnocentricity; on the other hand if they were to distance themselves from the controversy then they could be viewed as shirking their responsibility to ensure justice in the distribution of meal. What were they to do? Let us try to understand some aspects of the situation in which the apostles were caught.

The apostle on the day of Pentecost had forged a multiethnic and multilingual community where diversities was reconciled. This was diametrically opposite to the community of Israel which was acutely ethnocentric. The neonate community was composed as a sign of God's new way of working in the world through his Son, Jesus Christ. This new eclectic community was the manifestation that God's love which included Israel but expanded beyond its boundary to all the nations of the world. This is the first aspect.

The second aspect of this community was an urgent sense to care for its needy widows. For this new believers sold their properties and deposited the proceeds to the apostles. Their love for property was diminished in view of the belief in the imminent return of Christ. However, due to the delay in Christ's return the poor widows of the community needed to be fed. To sketch a complete picture of the situation in the distribution of food to widows it must be admitted the Jewish believers had inhibitions due to ritual purity. As a result of which the Greek widows must have been served food towards the end i.e., after the Jewish widows were all served; and the leftover food proved to be insufficient for the rest. At any rate the Greek widows were at a disadvantage. This was not only a matter of inefficient management but also an issue of social injustice. Keeping in view that all the apostles were Jewish and the disadvantaged widows were Greek, the apostles had carefully selected deacons from both Greek and Jewish backgrounds to serve the poor widows. They hoped that this arrangement would ensure impartiality and transparency. However, to restate the dilemma was it right for the apostles to distance themselves from the situation? Should they not have directly supervised the arrangement of food distribution?

In the Light of the Law

What must be appreciated is this that the care for widows which was an injunction of Mosaic Law was being universally applied in the neonate community. Its benefit were to reach both to the Hebrews and the Hellenics. This was what the Law stated,

> "At the end of every three years, bring all the tithes of that year's produce and store it in your towns, so that the Levites (who have no allotment or inheritance of their own) and the foreigners, the fatherless and the widows who live in your towns may come and eat and be satisfied, and so that the Lord your God may bless you in all the work of your hands." (Deuteronomy 14:28-29 NIV).

Notwithstanding the noble provisions of the Law, this case is an example of how a discrimination could rise due to some oversight which might have led to a failure of a well-intended arrangement. In this case it was the oversight of the care for the Hellenic widows.

Oversights can also happen in our contemporary social context if we are not alert about certain cultural practices. For example there could be a discriminatory practice against Dalit Christian women within the church. Needless to say that discrimination is already prevalent in the wider society.

In the Light of Gospel

As we have seen that the care for the widows as a matter of justice was already provided in the Mosaic Law. In the Gospel Jesus was clear that he had not come to abolish the law or the prophets but to fulfil them. This is what he said,

> "Therefore anyone who sets aside one of the least of these commands and teaches others accordingly will be called least in the kingdom of heaven, but whoever practices and teaches these commands will be called great in the kingdom of heaven." (Matthew 5:19).

It is clear from what Jesus has taught that the positive laws of taking care of the needy was not to be ignored. In the sermon of the mount this is what Jesus said,

> "So when you give to the needy do not announce it with trumpets... but when you give to the needy do not let your left hand know what your right hand is doing, so that your giving may be in secret." (Matthew 6:2&4).

In the light of God's Word let us try to address the dilemma which the people in the community face and what is our witness to it. It is true that we have worked with different groups of people and who have cooperated well in the society and communities but let us also see that how the early community witnessed to life in Christ.

In the socio-political setting of 30-70 CE dictatorial governance was prevalent. The Hebrews tended to be narrow and rigid, with few interests outside their own small world; the Hellenistic Jews were generally much more ready to recognize the better features of the wider Gentile world beyond the confines of the Promised Land. Tensions between Hebrews and Hellenists went back a long time, to the very beginnings of Greek domination when many Jews were hellenized. The brilliant world of Greek thought and culture burst upon the Jews and threatened to destroy Judaism, both with its philosophy and by its persecution. We read a record of it in the two books of Maccabees.

Amidst these conflicting ethnicities the apostles were promoting the ideals of an egalitarian society where everyone would be treated equal and share from the common purse. For the Jews both Hebrew and Hellenistic who had recently started to live together as a community it was important for the Apostles to ensure that it was to be a caring and a sharing community.

This was possible if Christ's emphasis on egalitarianism was taken seriously. The attractiveness of Christ's teaching was finally sealed on the Pentecost by the Holy Spirit. It must be noted that the emergence of neonate community was not an excluding event; rather it included diverse language groups constituting *reconciled diversity*. The early believers wanted to be a part of a community which would give them opportunities to flourish.

The keyword for *flourishing* was "happiness". This was an interior feeling of believing and belonging was the thrill of the members of this neonate community in Jerusalem. In words of the hymn writer George Wade Robinson

> Heav'n above is softer blue,
> Earth around is sweeter green!
> Something lives in every hue
> Christless eyes have never seen.

Were the members of the neonate community happy? That their number grew was an indication of hope and happiness. No doubt that initially there was no complaining, or criticisms, or envy, or strife. The members of the neonate community were all filled with the Holy Spirit and the evidence of which was visible in signs and wonders. This community was a company of people praising God, that is to say, they were a worshipping community.

The Lord added to their number daily who were being saved (Acts 2:47b). The community did not grow just by adding members through baptism but increased in numbers by the saving grace of God. The 'saving grace' brought about repentance, justice and acceptance which was the cause of the increase in the numbers of adherents, rather than daily rations or favors. People found neonate community to be free of xenophobia. There was hope and happiness among the members. Here we add that happiness was not mere contentment; rather it is an inner disposition of a person that results from experiencing justice.

Notwithstanding, that *happiness* is the key for flourishing community, the fact is that feeling of happiness does not always remain high. As a community grows larger so does its needs, and cynicism find its ways among its members, the cause of which could be injustice in the distribution of its resources. The murmuring or complaining resulting out of injustice, actual or perceived, can be either sowed or induced. When such complaints or complication surface, for instance in the Neonate community, some break their silence for those who may have silently suffered injustice, as was the case with Greek widows. In a multiethnic community sensitivity to others is important. If not detected in time, the cohesiveness of community is likely to be jeopardized.

The heterogeneous character of community was masked by diversity in their religious backgrounds, language and cultures. Thus causing inequality in participation in decision-making process and unequal treatment. As a result the graph of happiness index of the neonate community had gone down. The members of this neonate community who were deeply conditioned by the culture of purity laws, were unable to refocus on the new standard of relationship with other people. They needed to apply the new standard of "the law of love" instead of the old standard of "the law of purity and pollution" to forge relationships. To use Jesus's figure of speech: if the new wine was the neonate community, then its new wine-skin was the law of love.

Love is the companion of happiness. The neonate community was founded on teaching of Jesus which was love. In the neonate community, the two factions namely the Hebrew and Hellenist were trying to dissolve their difference and prejudices arising out of the laws of purity. Although they tried to cement their differences, soon complaints surfaced. To address the situation the apostles took a swift action.

It is important to note that love for one another is a key to surpass all differences. We, who have gathered here in Kolkata, are a heterogeneous community. We belong to diverse nation, speak diverse languages, follow diverse cultural norms; many of us are vocally dominant and others are forced to silence. The question before us should be this, we who are created in God's image, are we not to be enablers to make that sacred image shine forth in others? If that is so then are we not to implement the Nazareth Manifesto? (Luke 4:18).

It is important that we should be filled with His word, and words of encouragement. Paul says in 2 Timothy 2:15 "Do your best to present yourself to God as one approved, a worker who does not need to be ashamed and who correctly handles the word of truth." It is important to note that Jesus used words of encouragement for those who need it and those who practiced it. e.g. "Go your faith has healed you", "Sin no more", "I have never seen such faith in the house of Israel". For a community to grow in happiness it is important to encourage, love, care and maintain stability. Moreover the words of encouragement play significant role in an atmosphere of love. Love for one another develops a habit of co-existence.

It must be highlighted that a community enriches itself when it generously shares. For this the leaders of the community play a pivotal role. Concerning leadership St. Paul wrote, "So Christ himself gave the apostles, the prophets, the evangelists, the pastors and teachers, to equip his people for works of service, so that the body of Christ may be built up until we all reach unity in the faith and in knowledge of the Son of God and become mature, attaining to the whole measure of the fullness of Christ" (Ephesians 4:11-13).

The neonate community, despite its ideals, had its drawbacks. As time passed on and decades set in St. Paul had to remind the emerging communities what was expected of their leaders— apostles, prophets, evangelists, pastors and teachers. Besides being honest and committed they were expected to build capabilities of their communities. They were to be made capable to care and share, to learn and teach, to organize and administer the people. Along with personal commitment, the leaders were expected to be wise. An exemplary person for wisdom was King Solomon in the Hebrew scripture. He had asked God to give him a discerning heart to distinguish between right and wrong. God was pleased and gave him a wise and discerning heart (1Kings 3:9-12). In the same way God endowed primitive church leaders with wisdom and his Holy Spirit.

Clearly wisdom is an important ingredient for leadership. Leaders fail their communities to flourish if they fail in their exercise of wisdom. For example, when a progressive plan is proposed, it requires wisdom to plan out its implementation. A skilled leader could do that. Being filled with Holy Spirit, does not mean merely infused with *charisma*; rather the power to reason should also added to it. Being filled with wisdom refers to human capacity of insight, exercise of reasoning, inspiration of spirit and confidence in making decision. This blending will make a leader capable to lead his community to flourishment and happiness.

Luke in his book "Acts of the Apostles" gives a picture of this antique community. It was as imperfect as we are today. This shows the human side of the church and its struggles. The church has never been a perfect community. But it always had believers who strived to live in the perfection of Christ. They worshipped Christ as Lord, and as one who had changed their lives. It is important to note that the neonate community through their action pointed out that Christ mediated God's new covenant both through service and salvation.

The problems of the neonate community, in some way, is present in our church today. The Church Universal is divided into geographical, ethicnic, socio-economic and denominational segments. Moreover it can never assemble in one place at one time. There are people who are without food and yet we might never even know them. The chances of being overlooked is much greater today than it was in the days of the neonate community in Jerusalem. It is important to hold that a community's growth does not depend merely on relief work; instead it depends of various factors one of which is "belonging" and the other is "believing". Both these involve caring and sharing.

In this study we took the neonate community of the New Testament times into consideration. We appreciated their vision to forge a inclusive community of diverse ethnicities as a model for others to duplicate. The aim was to create "happiness" in their struggles for life. The basis for happiness was love. We discussed that love has a character to be unconditional crossing all ethnocentric boundaries.

The decades that followed after the formation of neonate community of the first believers as recorded in the *Acts of the Apostles*, needed to be reminded that the social diversity they had embraced in love, had reconciled all differences and had included all diversities. This was true also for the other early Christian communities which followed the pattern of neonate church. But something more was required to create happiness in the new community of Christians. We studied that happiness was the result of caring and sharing with the needy in the community.

Having studied these basic principles of flourishing community from the New Testament records, we have to apply it in our South Asian context today. The South Asian region is in post-colonial era. Many countries are democratic but others are not. There is diversity of religion, language and cultures. Added to this there is grinding poverty, desperate socio-economic inequaities and backwardness. In India we have to reckon with the torturous reality of caste-system.

Over and against the caste based society we are challenged to create two kinds of communities, one, the national community and two, the ecclesial community. Granted that every nation in South Asia must reconcile all social and cultural diversity to form a national community, nonetheless church's prophetic voice to advocate civil liberties and human rights should not be diluted. Therefore, *firstly*, with courage God's people have to stand for human right to liberty, life and property and against all forms for evil of dictatorial governments. In view of the fact that Buddhism, Hinduism, and Islam along with various regional practices shape up the social, political and cultural life of people, inter-religious dialogues must be given due impetus.

Secondly in all South Asian countries the ecclesial communities or the church should also be constituted on similar lines. Therefore various ecumenical endeavor must be given due impetus. Christian Churches in spite of their differences must engage in regular fellowship, Eucharistic hospitality and study of the Word of God.

Thirdly, among the south Asian countries what makes India, Pakistan, Bangladesh and Nepal peculiar is their practice of *varna vyavastha* or caste system which entails social inequality, segregation and untouchability against more than twenty percent of their population. In the face of this evil the church must engage in the prophetic ministry to speak out the truth against casteism. It entails concerted efforts for evangelizing both individuals and culture. In this context the women's concerns must not be underestimated. Granted that women of all sections are subjugated and silenced due to patriarchy, but the Dalit women are twice oppressed and the Dalit Christian woman is thrice—by being a woman, a Dalit and a minority. Caste is the greatest impediment for people to flourish.

At the end we should consider the dilemma of the apostles both sympathetically and critically. Our sympathy lies with their concern, as far as we can make out, to remain impartial by maintaining their distance. As Jewish men they did not desire to be seen as partisans of one group or the other. For this reason their decision not to directly involve themselves by delegating their responsibility to others was wise. However, our critical observation is that they withdrew from the situation of injustice without giving any verdict.

The lesson for us is to stick our heads out for the cause of justice even if it is inconvenient and may risk our reputation. A key for flourishing communities is the practice of *justice*. Here, I do not advocate social or ecclesial uniformity and centralized control over people rather my plea is to promote *reconciled-diversity*. In this way richness of diverse cultures and literatures will be available for mutual learning, enrichment and progress. This is foundational to make the communities flourish.

§ § §

Chapter 4

Principles for Flourishing: Stability and Harmony

Jeremiah had seen several governments which rose and fell. The reign of Josiah (640-609 BCE), Jehoahaz (609 BCE), Jehoakim (609-598 BCE), Jehoiachin (598-597 BCE) and Zedekiah (597-586 BCE). It is obvious that he had ministered more than 40 years from 627 BCE until 586 BCE when Jerusalem and the temple were destroyed and people went into exile in Babylonia (2Kings 25:21; 2 Chronicles 36:20). It must be noted that Jeremiah escaped being exiled but he went away to Egypt (Jeremiah 43:7&8) with the remnants of Judah. Jeremiah wrote a long communique to the Jews in Babylonia exiled by Nebuchadnezzar. The excerpt below is from this letter.

"This is what the Lord Almighty, the God of Israel, says to all those I carried into exile from Jerusalem to Babylon: "Build houses and settle down; plant gardens and eat what they produce. Marry and have sons and daughters; find wives for your sons and give your daughters in marriage, so that they too may have sons and daughters. Increase in number there; do not decrease. Also, seek the peace and prosperity of the city to which I have carried you into exile. Pray to the Lord for it, because if it prospers, you too will prosper." Yes, this is what the Lord Almighty, the God of Israel, says: "Do not let the prophets and diviners among you deceive you. Do not listen to the dreams you encourage them to have. They are prophesying lies to you in my name. I have not sent them," declares the Lord. This is what the Lord says: "When seventy years are completed for Babylon, I will come to you and fulfill my good promise to bring you back to this place. For I know the plans I have for you," declares the Lord, "plans to prosper you and not to harm you, plans to give you hope and a future." (Jeremiah 29:4-11)

It is clear in the text above that the Israelites were in a *fragile* condition in exile. Politically they were a defeated nation, culturally they were made inferior to the Persians, and as far as their religion was concerned they had nothing left except the ruins of their Temple in Jerusalem. In the conflict with the Persians the hand of Nebuchadnezzar was hard on them. Their elites were taken captive to Nineveh and the poor were left behind to till the land. The once flourishing community of the Israelites had vanished from their ancestral land.

In this fragile condition Jeremiah brings the message of hope. The people of Israel in spite of their fragile state must learn to flourish. With this in view Jeremiah wrote to them in a typical prophetic genre i.e. in dual authorship style. On the one hand the letter is written by Jeremiah and at the same time it is also God's words to his people. God spoke through his prophet without dictating his message. In a way Jeremiah was like God's secretary, who articulated the mind of God putting it down in his own words in writing. However, the message was clear that despite their fragile condition Israelites must learn to flourish.

Centuries have passed since prophet Jeramiah wrote this long message to the exiled Jews in Babylon, but his concerns are still relevant. The question for us is this, how do we flourish? How do we understand what human flourishing is and what is our contribution in it? In short a life that is lived well in *right relationship* with God, with environment and with neighbors is a sign of flourishing. However, *rightness of relationship* cannot be reduced merely to the riddance of certain feelings like guilt or shame. Granted that fostering healthy ideas in various fields of human interest are important but the key is response and adaptation to the changes in social environment. As Jeremiah had advised to the exiled Jews in his letter, we also should endeavor to flourish wherever we are.

From Fragile into Flourishing

Flourishing is an important aspect of development in an overall sense. The Bible not only provides values and vision for flourishing but it helps and enables us to pursue and experience flourishing. It is very important that a community must have specific goals and clarity on as to *why* they are living together. God's people, like every community, have a charter, which defines as to why its members are living together, albeit the reason for their existence is uniquely distinct. As theologian Jonathan Pennington argues,

> "Human flourishing is in fact a key biblical theme woven through the whole canon, one which, when recognized, explains and enhances some foundational aspects of the Bible's testimony, including the very nature and goal of God's redemption for us in Christ, who, after all, promises us eternal and abundant life. That is, the Bible, across its whole Christian canon of both Old and New Testament, is providing its own God-of-Israel-revealed-in-Jesus-Christ answer to the foundational human question of how to flourish and thrive."

An example of Biblical text on flourishing is Psalms 1:2-3. Concerning those who meditate on God's law it is said,

> "But they delight in the law of the LORD, meditating on it day and night. They are like trees planted along the riverbank, bearing fruit each season. Their leaves never wither, and they prosper in all that they do."

It is clear from the above text that God wants human beings to flourish. This was precisely what God spoke to his exiled people in Babylon through his prophet Jeremiah. His people were to settle down in Babylon and to start thinking about how they could make their life to flourish in the land of exile. In other words they needed to respond by adjusting and adapting themselves to their new social environment and changed political situation in order to advance materially and culturally.

Flourishing is another name for advancement. It has to be a continuous progress in line with time. In other words it denotes continuous adjustment and adaptation to changing social-political environment. In our times we must also add climatic change. In must be admitted that climatic changes occurs as nature takes a turn, but in our age it is induced by human activities of industry and technology. Unlike other animal species who adapt themselves to survive in their respective environments, human beings alter the environment to suit their survival. This human alterations in environment when excessive whether by air-conditioning or heating or building designed to suit our needs degrades the environment. For this reason climatic justice needs to be given due attention.

Thomas Jefferson, the third President of United States, articulated the three basic human needs: to live, to be free and to pursue happiness. Flourishing, therefore, is outwardly focused and is aimed to bring happiness and blessings to all. In the text of Jeremiah above we should not expect to see a formula for prosperity; rather we can deduce some basic principles to make communities flourish. We can deduce at least five basic principles from the text of Jeremiah we have taken for our study today. These are stable economy for self-reliance, stable family for social security, real local involvement for social harmony, collective resilience and the power of hope. Let us discuss each of these below.

Stable Economy for Self-reliance

Economic capacity is important for people to flourish. This capacity is dependent on two things firstly, on the capability of production secondly, capability of providing services. It is for this reason that Jeremiah advised people "to build and to plant" in their land of exile (Jeremiah 29:5). We should interpret the phrase "build houses" in a wider sense which should include developing infrastructures. Such facilities are important for the operation of common programs of a community which could be social, cultural, political or economic. As far as economic activity is concerned trading is its most important aspect. Therefore, the phrase "plant gardens and eat what they produce" should also be interpreted to include both production and trade. Quality in production and freedom in trade ensures a good turnover of economy which is fundamental for self-reliance of a community.

Granted that people who become dependent cannot flourish; the Jews in exile could at least become economically sufficient if not politically independent to flourish. Economic sufficiency comes with trade and business. A fundamental element in trade is trust. But it is difficult to trust strangers. Would the Babylonians trust the exiled Jews? It was important for the Jews to win the trust of Babylonians and also increase their population to become viable in producing goods to trade. With a viable population and production the Exiles could create trade networks both in their host-country as well as with their home-country. A way to earn the trust of Babylonians was to be subservient and not rebellious. Similarly to earn trust of the Israelites back home was to be loyal to Yahweh, who was God all the Israelites both in Babylon and Judah. Having gained trust, the exiles could receive cooperation and gain trading partners from a large geographical area.

Herein lies the economic principle of flourishing. Stable economy for self-reliance not only ensures that the needs of all the members of the community are met with the exchange of currency, but also that a community is capable to provide services and goods to meet the needs of other people whether far or near, friends or foes, neighbors or strangers. This *trust* is not only to be shared in history but also in the value of currency and standard of measurements. This is an absolute requisite to flourish despite fragile condition.

Stable Family for Social Security

The primary net for social security for human beings is their family. Jeremiah understood this social fact very well. He was anxious for the survival of the Israelites in exile. If they lost enthusiasm to live it could lead annihilation of the whole people. Jeremiah's anxiety was not unfounded for example the exiled community were capable of composing Psalm 137 which laments

> By the rivers of Babylon we sat and wept
> When we remembered Zion.
> There on the poplars
> We hung our harps,
> For there our captors asked us for songs,
> Our tormentors demanded songs of joy;
> They said, "Sing us one of the songs of Zion!"
> How can we sing the song of the Lord while in a foreign land?

There might have many such songs, however, people could not be surrendered to mental depression.

A tragic historical example is of the native Tasmanians who had survived for 10,000 years in splendid isolation. But within one hundred years they were completely wiped out to the last man, woman and child with Captain James Cook's arrival on the island. European settlers first drove them out of the fertile parts of the island then in greed of the remaining wilderness they hunted them down and killed them systematically. A few survivors were helped by some missionaries, who were well meaning but not open minded. They tried to modernize these native people of Tasmania in their mission camps. They instructed them in reading and writing, sewing clothes and farming. But the people refused to learn. They became ever more melancholic, stopped having children, lost all interest in life, and finally chose the only escape route from the modern world of science and progress—it was death.

Alas, they were pursued even after death. Their dead bodies were ceased by scientists and anthropologists. They were dissected, weighed and measured, and analyzed in learned articles. Their skulls and skeletons were displayed in museums. Only in 1976 did the Tasmanian Museum gave up for burial the skeletons of Truganini the last Tasmanian, who had died a hundred year earlier. The English Royal College of Surgeons held on to the samples of skin and hair till 2002 [HYN 2014:310]. This is the story of Truganini who died in depression deprived of family.

This tragedy should never befall any people. One good thing about the Jewish exiles was that they were not slaves in Babylon. This was the silver lining on a dark cloud. Therefore, Jeremiah advised the exiles to marry and to have children so that God's people would increase in number (Jeremiah 29:6). Note the emphasis in the verse "do not decrease". This phrase should be viewed in two ways: one, to increase in numbers in Exile; and two, to sustain enthusiasm in life. Thus, it is important that human beings should live in families and communities which can provide them companionship and social security in times of difficulties, disease and calamities.

Real Local Involvement for Social Harmony

Local involvement in a real sense means to become organic. This denotes putting down roots in culture and society. In other words getting associated with people and environment. Such association fosters security, social connection, emotional well-being, personal relationship, opportunities and access to resources. Jeremiah was aware that the exiles in Babylon were not going to return to their homeland in the near future. Therefore they were not to be given false hopes of return which could lead social maladjustment of the Exiles with the Babylonians. As a fragile community it was important that the Exiles lived in harmony with people around them.

Accordingly it was unwise for them to be confined in ghettos instead they needed to be involved in the local life of the wider society in Babylon. They had to learn how to be in social harmony with the wider society and yet keep their distinct identity as Jews. Jeremiah, therefore advise them "to seek the peace and prosperity of the city" (Jeremiah 29:7). This can only become a reality when different segments of community interact with one another in trade and governance in every local city. For this reason the members of every community must exist for causes beyond their own social boundaries. Flourishing of a community is evident when the involvement of its members brings beneficial transformation in the wider society. Saint Mother Teresa of Kolkata had once said,

> "I alone cannot change the world but I can cast a stone across water
> to create many ripples."

It is powerful saying which signifies the action of an individual member in the community. In a flourishing community it is important to understand that the action of every individual is important for social synergy and the uniqueness of each individual is very important to make that ripple. As the African word "Ubuntu" means "I am because we are" expresses the essential quality of being human. In a similar way Jesus in his Sermon on the Mount taught people to transform themselves for the benefit of others. He said "in everything, do to others what you would have them do to you" (Matthew 7:12). The reason for this is the simple fact that human beings along with other living beings and environment are interconnected and interdependent. Flourishing results when harmony in all relationships are restored. Nicholas Wolterstorff says,

> "A flourishing life is neither merely an 'experimentally satisfying
> life' as nor is it simply a life 'well-lived,' as a majority of ancient
> Western philosophers have claimed."

A healthy community is like a magnet, people come there and make their commitments. Flourishing community should not be compared with an efficient place of work. It is the welcoming nature and openness to other communities makes it a flourishing one. The health of community is measured by its welcome of the unexpected and simplicity of relationships among its members.

Further in light of what Jeremiah writes the importance of awareness and action should be highlighted. Awareness is enhanced by getting involved and getting connected with other the concerns of other local communities. The treasures of the kingdom—justice, peace and integrity of creation—are shared with other local communities. The implication of this is enrichment of micro-units. In other words every individual be aware of being related to a larger sphere. He or she will be aware how a local problem is a by-product or a result of a global problem. This awareness will enable them to draw up a proper strategy to bring the social transformation. In other words a strategy for progress from particular to general and from micro-level to macro-level. This principle of local involvement to enrich people and to enable strategic action helps to forge flourishing communities.

Collective Resilience

Granted that Nebuchadnezzar had defeated Judah, destroyed Jerusalem and exiled the Israelites but that did not mean annihilation of God's people. Though defeated they had the capacity to recover. This is the power of collective resilience. Jeremiah points out to the Israelites that their faith neither should depend on external signs like residing in the land nor should it depend on the existence of the Temple or the offering of the sacrifices. Rather the existence of God's people depended on God's faithfulness to them. He builds their confidence by bringing them the promise of God,

> "When seventy years are completed for Babylon I will come to you and fulfil my good promise to bring you back to this place."
> (Jeremiah 29:10).

With this hope in a bright future they could flourish in the present times even in the land of exile. But this promise for a bright future has a wider significance. It gave the exiled community and a defeated nation a collective confidence. This was the key for Jewish resilience. Hence, the feature of collective resilience is a mark of a flourishing community. The Psalmist says in 92:12-13,

> "The righteous will flourish, they will grow....planted in the house of the LORD, they will flourish in the courts of our God. They will still bear fruit in old age; they will stay fresh and green."

Resilience therefore is the fruit of moral power. It encompasses all our being, community is a place for practicing our ethics, which involves the practice of forgiving and doing justice which is the fruit of love. It is in such atmosphere that confidence is built up which is foundation for resilience. Only in a resilient community celebration, growth and liberation can take place. Every individual in a resilient community has the capability to create an atmosphere of peace and joy.

Resilience of a community depends on how much it members trust each other. Trust is that quality which creates a liberal environment for individuals to flourish. In biblical flourishing there are no special group but every individual who belongs to a community that is fragile has a opportunity to develop the power of resilience. In the Indian scenario it would be *Dalit* and *Adivasi, and* in South Asia scenario it could religious or ethnic or gender minorities. The inspiration is in Paul's letter to the Galatians,

> "There is neither Jew nor Gentile, neither slave nor free, nor is there male and female, for you are all one in Christ Jesus." (Galatians 3:28)

This means that power of resilience is available to every individual and every community.

The second essential quality for resilience is love which should be taken as seriously as trust. The model of love for members of the community is Jesus who on the night that he was betrayed washed the feet of his disciples. But at the same time we also need to learn to accept our own essential nature. We find trust when we accept our human condition with all its limitations, and then search for happiness resolutely ready to follow Christ and to rise to the challenges of life. It is essential to know that when a community is born it heals the pain of loneliness and wounds of seclusion of each person who accepts Jesus.

Power of Hope

The power of hope is a common desire of a community which attracts its members who aim beyond their private concerns and unite to achieve the common goal. The power of hope radically reverses the thinking of the people to become selfless. In other words its members make the transition in their attitude i.e. from 'the community for myself' to 'myself for the community'. It is for this reason that Jeremiah forbids people to listen to such prophets and diviners who preach ethnocentric message. Their messages encouraged social exclusivity which could ghettoize the people. In contrast to this God's message to his people through Jeremiah was to seek peace and prosperity for Nineveh to which he had carried them in exile, and pray for its prosperity. "Because if it prospers, you too will prosper" said the Lord (Jeremiah 29:7b).

Some of us would like to see in this a movement from the culture of death to the culture of life. This movement is made possible by the power of hope. We may also be reminded of Sermon on the Mount where Christ speaks of human flourishing of happiness in the beatitudes. Each beatitude has a promise which also is a hope, for example in the fragile situation of conflict the peacemakers are blessed because they have a hope to be called the children of God (Matthew 5:8). For a fragile community hope is the power to generate flourishing.

The prophet warns the Exiles from being fooled by false hope. They were not to be deceived by false prophets or diviners who proclaimed only empty dreams of returning to the land of Judah. With the hope of a better future they were to find their *welfare* in the welfare of Babylon. Therefore, he advised them to pray for the welfare of Babylon. This is a remarkable facet of the prophet who because of such convictions was hated by his own people. Despite God's vengeance on them the prophet builds up their confidence to face the political reality of prolonged time of exile. He brings them hope of eventual emancipation which still was far into the future. Even though the well-being of the Exiles was bound up with the welfare of Babylon, this is in part a reaching forward to that later words of Jesus,

> "You have heard that it was said, 'Love your neighbor and hate your enemy.' But I tell you, love your enemies and pray for those who persecute you, that you may be children of your Father in heaven. He causes his sun to rise on the evil and the good, and sends rain on the righteous and the unrighteous. If you love those who love you, what reward will you get? Are not even the tax collectors doing that? And if you greet only your own people, what are you doing more than others? Do not even pagans do that? Be perfect, therefore, as your heavenly Father is perfect." (Matthew 5:43-48).

It is the power of hope which gives rise to the radical perspective of the teachings of Christ. The view point is revolutionary.

We have studied five principles of *Flourishing Communities* in fragile situation these were based on biblical text of Jeremiah. The principles were: stable economy, stable family, local involvement, collective resilience and the power of hope. These principles were qualified by trust and love. We saw that trust in one another was a basic ingredient for stable economy. Similarly love for one another was the basic ingredient for resilience. In fact both the qualities of love and trust were part of ethical qualities from Christian prospective.

We learned that stable economies created self-reliance among people, stable families created a network for social security, real local involvement was fundamental to forge social harmony, moral power was necessary for collective resilience and the power of hope was important for radical transformation and consolation of distressed people in fragile conditions.

In all this which constitutes ingredients for *Flourishing Community*, true flourishing only comes with the prevalence of justice. The Law of Moses clearly captures the heartbeat of God in the following injunction.

> "Follow justice and justice alone, so that you may live and possess the land the Lord your God is giving you." (Deuteronomy 16:20).

Justice in the above text must be understood in the wider sense to include gender and climate justice. Much needs to be explored on the subject of Flourishing Communities which is beyond the scope of this study. But what we have learned is this that every individual is called to flourish by relating to other individuals and to create an environment of justice and righteousness; and that every human community needs to share its culture, resources, preferences, needs and other commonalities with others; and that human beings must pursue climatic justice despite adapting and adjusting to the changing socio-political and natural environment. Let me close this bible study with a quote of Chinua Achebe, a Nigerian novelist,

> "While we do good works let us not forget that the real solution lies in which charity will have become unnecessary."

This vision is the power of our hope to make human beings flourish in harmony with the natural environment. But this cannot be the last word on this subject.

§ § §

References

[HYN] Harari. Yuvan Noah, *"Sapiens"* (2014) Vintage London.

Chapter 5

Moving Ahead to Flourish

There is no doubt that caste system is the greatest hindrance for communities in India to *flourish*. The binaries of touchable and untouchables, segregation and untouchability, clean and unclean, antipathy and cooperation, endogamy and exogamy among the castes interlocks all competing castes into symbiotic relationship. The tension among the binaries does not result in revolution but stratification. It must be admitted that a stratified society does not flourish in the sense of *advancement* that is to say, by adapting and adjusting to the changing environment.

It is clear from the above discussion that caste and patriarchy has made our community and society fragile. Therefore, one way is to correct the situation is to annihilate them. Set free from these two hindrances the hitherto fragile communities will become free to flourish. But this is not possible in view of the fact that these ideas and their practices are deeply ingrained in people's psyche. But we cannot leave things at that. We must continue to analyse and theologise in the context of fragile conditions of our communities.

The iron hand of caste has ruthlessly subjugated large communities reducing them to become increasingly fragile. In the present context we have Dalit, Adivasi and women. As far as the minorities are concerned they are a part and parcel of the above three categories. To this we can add a list of other categories like the differently-abled people, LGBTIQ communities, elderly, children, COVID-19 patients, unorganized and unskilled labourers, people affected by leprosy and HIV/AIDS patients. All these people and communities are marked as fragile.

The experience of being fragile involves becoming brittle leading to the possibility of becoming broken people. Enabling needed to be taken urgently before disintegration occurs in an irreversible manner. Granted that Dalit communities are broken people and Adivasi are a defeated or beaten people, they have not been reduced to irreversible condition of being annihilated. They are fragile but not shattered. Their population, language, culture and knowledge can be saved and made to flourish once more.

Therefore, at this point let us theologise using categories of fragility to flourishing from the perspective of Dalit and Adivasi communities. To begin with let us accept the fact that both communities experience fragility in several ways. By being silenced, alienated, and deprived of opportunities to be educated to earn money, food, shelter and medicines. This ensures that their impulse of organising themselves and agitating against oppression is curbed. All these can be further unpacked and elaborated. But first let us theologise.

Flourishing of Creation

God makes human beings to flourish out of fragility. Let us read a text of the Bible.

> "The LORD God formed a man from the dust of the ground and breathed into his nostrils the breath of life, and the man became a living being." (Genesis 2.7-8).

The 'dust of the ground' denotes the fragile condition, conversely 'living being' represents flourishing condition. As we understand, God wants all creation to flourish. Granted that God created everything out of nothing, but what came into existence was fragile material of earth and water,

> "Now the earth was formless and empty, darkness was over the surface of the deep, and the Spirit of God was hovering over the waters." (Genesis 1.2).

God did not allow this fragile chaos of water-covered earth to disintegrate; instead He gave rise to an ordered universe to of flourish in six days. It shows that fragility has within it the potential to flourish. God works on fragile things making them to flourish.

In the first creation narrative we see that God in his creative power moves forward in progressive manner—from nothing He creates everything to flourish. In the second narrative we read God's creative activity progressing from creation of inorganic material to create organic life, culminating human beings, namely, Adam and Eve possessing intelligent consciousness. In both narratives the progress is from fragile condition to flourishing conditions.

The second creation narrative unfolds the condition of Adam as being fragile in loneliness in the vegetated earth of the plant kingdom. The LORD God said, "It is not good for man to be alone. I will make a helper suitable for him." (Genesis 2.18). Here loneliness creates a fragile condition for Adam in a comprehensive way involving social, emotional and biological aspects. Then God addressed Adam's fragile condition and created the animal kingdom from the ground. But Adam, though superior to animals possessing the power to name other creatures, could not properly flourish in the environment of plants and animals, till Eve was created. She was created out of Adam's rib denoting her to be equal in stature, in splendour, in ability and dignity. Adam flourished with her as together their fecundity came into full play of fertility.

Flourishing in God's good creation is not merely to live in a static fashion; it entails dynamism i.e. to live productively. In other words, a creature who is able to live, reproduce and nurture its offspring is indicative of a flourishing organism. This organic reality is also applicable to human community. A community which lives, increases and cultivates its culture, is a flourishing community.

The biblical narratives starts from individuals and develops into a community. The way the elected ones of God flourish overcoming their fragility, is similar to a community which flourishes by overcoming its instability.

Flourishing of Noah

We know the story of Noah and the deluge. There is a detailed description of the fragile condition of the world of that time. This is how it is described,

> "So God said to Noah, 'I am going to put an end to all people, for the earth is filled with *violence* because of them. I am surely going to destroy both them and the earth. So make yourself an ark … I am going to bring floodwaters on the earth to destroy all life under the heavens, every creature that has the breath of life in it. Everything on earth will perish.' " (Genesis 6.13-14a; 17).

Due to *violence* suggesting excessive slaughter of animals and killings of human beings in the internecine conflicts, the human society and biological nature sunk into fragility. Both were destroyed except the members of Noah's family and the animals in the ark. Despite the impending destruction by deluge the LORD God promised that,

> "But I will establish my covenant with you, and you will enter the ark—you and your sons and your wife and your sons' wives with you" (Genesis 6.18).

After the experience of being fragile—adrift on the waters on a lone ark with his family and animals finding himself helpless as the rest of living creatures fell to destruction—Noah experienced salvation. After the rain had stopped the dove returned to the ark with a fresh plucked olive leaf in its beak. Flood had receded from the earth, and land had appeared (Genesis 8.13). Then in response to Noah's sacrifice of thanksgiving God promised,

> "As long as the earth endures,
> Seedtime and harvest,
> Cold and heat,
> Summer and winter,
> Day and night
> Will never cease." (Genesis 8.22).

In this cosmic covenant lay God's promise of universal flourishing, that is to say, that God's providential governance and earth's sustaining provision for all living creatures would never cease. Accordingly God blessed Noah and his sons saying to them,

> "Be fruitful and increase in number and fill the earth." (Genesis 9.1).

This is an example of a fragile condition caused by violence, which adversely affected the earth and Noah's family. The destruction by deluge was the divine punishment on human wickedness; and yet God brought both the earth and Noah's family to flourish.

Flourishing of Patriarchs

The three patriarchs—Abraham, Isaac and Jacob—started their lives in fragile conditions. They all were nomadic clans without a land of their own. Abraham was childless even till the old age. With no offspring and no land to settle, despite the wealth of cattle and servants, Abraham was a broken man. His flourishing, however, came through Sarah his wife, who bore him a son, Isaac, in their old age. This son born of God's promise was a sign of hope and support to them. The hope to flourish which became a reality in their old age was with a purpose. Using anthropomorphic style the narrative moves forward,

> Then the LORD said, "Shall I hide from Abraham what I am about to do? Abraham will surely become a great and powerful nation, and all nations on earth will be blessed through him. For I have chosen him, so that he will direct his children and his household after him to keep the way of the LORD by doing what is *right* and *just*, so that the LORD will bring about for Abraham what he has promised him." (Genesis 18.19).

The promise of flourishing for the nomadic patriarch was not merely to biologically populate the earth, but to promote *righteousness* and *justice*. They would flourish for the cause of establishing morality among the nations. Hence in God's plan flourishing is tied up with morality. In the absence of morality starting with the murder of Abel till the time of Noah and in the land of Shinar, the biblical history narrates how human communities got crippled with violence, wickedness and unnatural sex ending in their annihilation by flood.

That the principle of moral order demanded this extreme measure from the author of moral law indicates the gravity of immoral situation. The result of immorality was destruction. Hence the author expressed it as,

> "So God said to Noah. "I am going to put an end to all people for the earth is filled with *violence* because of them. I am surely going to destroy both them and the earth." (Genesis 6.13).

In the larger plan of God to save the world from extinction he had commanded Noah and his family with pairs of all clean and unclean animals to enter the ark.

After the destruction by deluge the remnant of creatures that came out of the ark were in fragile condition. There were no cities, no farms, no livestock, no craftsman, no black smith, no industry, and no infrastructure of any sort. It is from this fragile condition that they built their first city Babel, which alas they got it wrong, till under the guidance of God Abraham would set things right. The divine guidance for successful flourishing was the firm stick of morality—to do right and to be just.

To reverse the fragile situation God called Abram, renamed Abraham, with the promise to flourish,

> "The LORD had said to Abram, "Go from your father's household to the land I will show you.
>
> > I will make you into a great nation,
> > And I will bless you;
> > I will make your name great,
> > And you will be a blessing.
> > I will bless those who bless you,
> > And whoever curses you I will curse;
> > *And all peoples of the earth will be blessed through you."*
>
> (Genesis 12.1-3)

Attention should be drawn to the reversal from violence to blessing. God's intention was to reverse the 'cycle of violence' to 'flourishing of blessing' on earth. For this Abraham was God's instrument because he positively responded to God's call.

Abraham in obeying God starts with a fragile condition of becoming nomadic and childless, and eventually becomes a wealthy man with an offspring of promise. His story is a paradigm for the salvation history of the whole creation. Starting with fragile condition—murder of Abel (Gen 4.8), vagabond condition of Cain (Gen 4.13*f*), high mortality (Gen 5), deviant sexual practices of human with non-human (Gen 6.4), conflict (Gen 14), violence and wickedness (Gen 6.11*f*). This is what the author of Genesis wrote,

> "The LORD saw how great the *wickedness* of the human race had become on the earth, and that every inclination of the thoughts of the human heart was only *evil* all the time." (Genesis 6.4).

The wickedness i.e. immoral acts of sex and violence was the root of exterminations of peoples—Canaanites and Jebusites; and destruction of cities of ancient times—Sodom and Gomorrah. It was over and against this fragile condition due to immorality which caused destruction, decay and death that God begins to shape his plans to make human communities flourish once again.

In a similar way we can read the histories of Isaac and Jacob. How they from their fragile conditions rose up to flourishing conditions. The author of Genesis intended to show that this was according to God's plan. Notwithstanding their fragile conditions due to their mistakes (Gen 38.12-26) conflicts (Gen 14) and fear (Gen 20.1-13), the history of God's people manifested who God was. It is clear from its reading that God intended to make life flourish in all forms and species, whether human or non-human.

Flourishing of Joseph

In this context the story of Joseph is most impressive. He was Jacob's son who was the third Hebrew patriarch. His story is a complete narrative from fragile to flourishing condition. Joseph himself was in a weak condition when he was handed over to the Arabs who in turn sold him in the slave-market in Egypt. Bought by Potiphar, he had an unfortunate episode with his wife. Being vulnerable he was not able to defend himself and was imprisoned.

The story discloses his weak and vulnerable condition as a slave, an accused and a prisoner in the foreign land of Egypt. Disinherited by his brothers, lost to his father, forgotten by Pharaoh's chief cupbearer, Joseph was in a personal way more fragile than anyone else, yet he was saved from being destroyed. Eventually he was rescued and restored to a very flourishing position. But the story does not end here. He became instrumental to restore the chain of food supply to his family, i.e. the Hebrew clan, who were languishing in famine. This involved a long track of investigation. Joseph, who became second to Pharaoh, had to test his brothers, conceal his identity from them, had to become confident of their attitude who had once sold him off to slavery and maintain his self-esteem even as he broke down in tears when he revealed himself to his brothers.

The episode ends on a happy note. The whole community of his brothers, which hitherto fragile due to famine and migration, began to flourish in the land of Goshen. The reason was that three things were restored between Joseph and his brothers i.e. relationship, confidence and dignity. Joseph began to trust his brothers; he developed greater confidence in them as they enabled him to reunite with his aged father; and Joseph did not disrespect them in spite of what that they had done to him. We can go on in a similar way to study the whole bible from the perspective of fragile conditions and flourishing communities. We hope that the above example serves as a paradigm to reread the bible from the fragile condition of Dalit, Adivasi and women.

The above examples which have been used to explain fragile versus flourishing conditions are from the book of Genesis of the Hebrew Scriptures. Let us also have an example from the New Testament.

Flourishing of Neonate Community

The first company of witnesses were formed into a 'school' to educate those believers who were enrolled by baptism. This was not a new idea in itself. Plato had founded an Academy in Athens and so did Gamaliel the Jewish Rabbi. The first enrolment of was three thousand international believers, which was an impressive number for the 'school' to begin with. They had a common time-table of study, meals and prayers. Those enrolled were to understand the new social design of divine governance according to the gospel of Jesus Christ; the aim and object of which was to make the social order of the new believers into a sacred order.

The new social order was first designed as a small community of heterogeneous people, who started to live as a community of free and equal people intermingling at common meals of thanksgiving. The practice of circumcision which was the basic cause to create social divisions by promoting untouchability, segregation or inequalities was replaced by baptism. The newly initiated experienced a sense of flourishing as a community as they lived, learnt, prayed and ate together. The crucial question before them was this, could this social design of unity be made sacred and a universal order?

Those who belonged to the *Way*, as the believers were called in the early phase of the New Testament times, lived in a fragile world which seemed at the verge of breaking down. The political and economic structures were exploitative.

For instance, the political system applied power in a descending order i.e. from the Roman Caesar way down to the foot soldier. The objective was to control people, resources and production. Conversely the economic system was designed to facilitate the flow of wealth upward i.e. from rural peasants at grassroots to urban Rome. Accordingly import and export taxes were imposed. Added to these was the Temple Tax. It was clear that people bore heavy burden of taxes. A glimpse of this is recorded in Matthew 17.24-27.

> "After Jesus and his disciples arrived in Capernaum, the collectors of the two-drachma temple tax came to Peter and asked, "Doesn't your teacher pay the temple tax?"
>
> "Yes, he does," he replied.
>
> When Peter came into the house, Jesus was the first to speak, "What do you think Simon?" he asked, "From whom do the kings of the earth collect duty and taxes—from their own children or from others?"
>
> "From others," Peter answered.
>
> "Then the children are exempt," Jesus said to him. "But so that we may not cause offense, go to the lake and throw out your line. Take the first fish you catch; open its mouth and you will find a four-drachma coin. Take it and give it to them for my tax and yours."

Jesus offered an alternative i.e. to find the money in the mouth of a fish. We do not know whether or not Peter did actually follow Jesus' suggestion. However, the tone of the dialogue reveals that the Temple tax was burdensome on people.

Injustice, at the time of Jesus was, ingrained into the social fabric through social, economic, political and religious structures and systems in Palestine. Very few questioned the source of injustice. The victims of injustice were called sinners. The prostitutes and the tax-collectors were the untouchables.

Economic poverty of the poor was regarded as victim's ancestral sins. For instance it is recorded in John 9.1-3,

> "As Jesus went along, he saw a man blind from birth. His disciples asked him, "Rabbi, who sinned, this man or his parents, that he was born blind?"

> Neither this man nor his parents sinned," said Jesus."

Jesus, however, made a sharp distinction between the *perpetuators* of unjust socio-religious structures and the *victims* of it. The result was that society was desperately unequal. The *perpetuators* of inequality were the Pharisees, the Scribes, lawyers, the rich people and kings. Whereas the *victims* were the tax-collectors, the prostitutes, sinners, the foreigners, the poor, the adulteress, people affected with leprosy and women.

Besides this, the society of those times was also very unequal and divided. There were slaves versus their masters, the privileged few versus large disadvantaged masses, rich versus the poor, elites versus crowds, dominant versus subjected people, victorious versus the vanquished. This inequality, which was perpetuated by unjust social structures, made the populace fragile and divided. To wait for the society to change and to flourish with justice was farfetched. Therefore, for individuals to find a way out of this was to strengthen their communities. One such community was the newly founded *ecclesia* church of Jesus Christ. The members of the *ecclesia* church were empowered by the risen and ascended Christ and His gift of the Holy Spirit which made them one.

However, we need to identify some leading principles from the biblical history albeit taken only from the book of Genesis. The question is this, what can enable communities to flourish. Flourishing includes salvation, liberation, emancipation, justice, righteousness and freedom. All these are loaded theological terms and can be significantly unpacked. We might not be able to do this in this here due to the constraint of space. But what we learn is this, that it is important to build flourishing communities particularly where structures of wider society is fragile and vulnerable due to conflict, division and poverty. Under such conditions wider society takes a long time to gain political and economic stability; whereas in the meanwhile a *community* can meet the needs of her members.

The fundamental principle of community be love and discipline of organised life which unites all her members as in moral order of equality, fellowship and liberty.

It must be admitted that the prospects for Dalit to escape from the vicious cycle of inequality, untouchability, segregation, occupation brokenness division and poverty is limited due to the prevalence of the caste system. The civic amenities and social services are greatly lacking and mostly non-existent in the rural residential sections of Dalit. It is in such conditions that flourishing communities are a fundamental prerequisite to creating the basic conditions for human dignity and flourishing.

§ § §

References

[RAS] Rathore. Aakash Singh, *Ambedkar Preamble: A Secret History of the Constitution of India* (2020) Vintage Penguin Books. Gurugram.

Chapter 6

Building Flourishing Communities

Due to the rise of Sociology in 1838 with Auguste Comte's (1798-1857) *The Law of Three Stages*, the focus shifted to scientific study of society. As community was taken as a subset of society its importance diminished. What was sometimes forgotten is this that no individual directly becomes a member of the society; instead individuals become members of society through the associations of their communities, for example through a Church or a academia or an institute.

In this study we have attempted to bring community back into focus. We pointed out that community and society are related but distinct, and that human beings live in both these modes. We learnt that to understand community in the Indian context is both interesting and dismal. This is so due to the Caste System which makes everything complicated whether it is the larger society or a community or the practices of patriarchy or feminism.

It is under these social conditions that the idea of *Flourishing Communities* has to be studied. The opposite of flourishing is to be *fragile*. At a social level it involves the experience of becoming brittle i.e. leading to the possibility of breaking up or even complete annihilation. Such broken people need urgent help before their social disintegration become irreversible. It is obvious that Dalit communities in our context are broken people and Adivasi are a defeated or beaten people. They have become fragile but are not annihilated. They can be saved from obliteration from the earth—this involves their language, songs, stories, dances, cuisine, attires, art and various other things of their culture.

In this regard we studied the leading features of *Caste System* and the nature of *casteist patriarchy*. Admittedly they live in communities, but that does not mean that they were flourishing. Communities could be stagnant in a stratified society. In this regard we found that these two i.e. Caste System and Patriarchy, were the chief hindrance to biblical social morality of egalitarianism, freedom and fellowship which are the three characteristics of justice. Although communities do offer good scope for individuals to flourish but on the whole no community would properly flourish in an unjust society.

Indian society is organized according to Caste System. Hence the communities are placed above and below each other in graded unequal fashion. Similarly occupations are fixed for each community in its caste, and caste is fixed by birth in which one is born. The horrendous aspect of caste system is untouchability and segregation which are basic practices based on false notion social inequality. Yet between the members of 'touchable' and 'untouchable' castes there is toleration and expulsion simultaneously. This is how dominant castes treat the scheduled castes. Thus communities in each caste are locked in with no possibility for upward mobility.

We discussed that it was possible to restructure human societies, and that there was no society that was divinely fated to be unchangeable—whether *Ecclesia* of the New Testament, or *Sangha* of Buddha, or *Ummah* of Islam or *Varna* of Sanatana dharma. In this regard we studied Dr Ambedkar's response to Bertrand Russell's article *Reconstruction of Society*. He underscored the importance of human impulse to act. But these impulses could be modified by *circumstances* in the social environment. These circumstances could be assessed for forging beneficial or harmful societies. Those circumstances which were assessed to be harmful were to be eliminated; conversely those which were beneficial could be promoted. A just reconstruction of society by elimination of adverse circumstances was extremely important for making communities to flourish.

Economics also played a positive role in the reconstruction of society which eventually effects communities. Without taking the role of wealth—its creation and circulation and regulation— seriously, no society would progress and no community flourish. In Dr Ambedkar's view, money was not an end in itself; instead it was a *means* to an end. Money would be evil if the end was evil and good if the end was good, yet money was important to build a just community of free and equal people.

Building a Just Community of Free and Equal People

Can we build communities of free and equal people? And to ensure that communities as a whole are free from the domination of other communities? And that all communities relate to each other with equity and at par with other communities in the larger society?

In this regard Samuel Shekhar in his two Bible Studies (Chapters 3 and 4) has presented us with *foundations* and *principles* for Flourishing Communities. He underscored that these foundations are *reconciled-diversity* and *justice*. A homogeneous or unequally structured community has limited chance to progress. He did an exposition of Acts 6.1-7 concerning the distribution of food to the widows in the neonate community in Jerusalem where the Greek-speaking widows were overlooked. It was a matter of injustice in a community that was founded by reconciling all diversities. Here he discussed distributive and restorative aspects of justice. Mere contentment without justice brings no happiness.

In his second study he highlighted that for flourishing communities principles of stability and harmony were important. He did an exposition of Jeremiah 29.4-11 concerning the life of Jewish exiles in Babylon. Instead of wiling away their time in daydreaming, or licking wounds of defeat, or getting frustrated they needed to put down their roots in the foreign land and work hard to produce, trade and settle well in Babylon. In other words, they needed determination to adapt and adjust themselves in a new environment. To do this was important to survive. Unless they survived the hardship of exile there would be no hope for them to flourish as a community in the future.

Finally we did some more theologising and discovered a relationship between the flourishing of God, individuals and communities in the biospheres of God's creation. Flourishing of organic life is a metaphor of the flourishing of social life. We saw that in the Biblical narratives there is a progressive movement of flourishing from particular to universal, in other words, from individuals like Joseph to community like Israel. In this line of revelation we briefly studied Creation, Patriarchs in the Old Testament, and the neonate community of New Testament times.

We highlighted how Jesus distinguished between the *perpetuators* of unjust socio-religious structures and the *victims* of it. In other words Jewish community was divided into desperately unequal sections. The Pharisees, the Scribes, lawyers, the rich people and kings *perpetuated* social inequality. Whereas the *victims* were the tax-collectors, the prostitutes, sinners, the foreigners, the poor, the adulteress, the children, people affected with leprosy and women.

Besides this, the larger society of those times was also very unequal. There were slaves versus their masters, few privileged versus large disadvantaged masses, rich versus the poor, elites versus crowds, dominant versus subjected people, victorious versus the vanquished. This inequality, which was perpetuated by unjust social structures, made the populace fragile. To wait for the society to change and to flourish with justice was farfetched. Therefore, a way out for the individuals was to strengthen their communities. One such community was the newly founded *ecclesia* church of Jesus Christ. The members of the *ecclesia* church were empowered by the risen and ascended Christ and His gift of the Holy Spirit.

The Kirk and the Polis

In the foreword, Solomon George, had pointed out that in the caste ridden social condition the people of dominant castes have manipulated and monopolised places and resources in the larger society. As a result of which the so called 'low' castes and the Dalit community have very limited space to flourish or expand. In this condition of social stagnation the idea to form *Flourishing Community* is a recovery of focus on community life. Church or *Kirk* is one such community and *polis or city* is another. In this section I have used two words *Kirk* denoting life in church, and *Polis* denoting life in city. Both *Kirk* and *Polis* are crisp words for two communities to which people separately and simultaneously belong.

Therefore, for our purpose we should regard *Kirk* and *Polis* in the widest sense. *Kirk* includes local churches and congregations to national synods and global bodies like World Council of Churches and Papacy. Similarly *Polis* includes city councils and village panchayats at the local levels, and Legislative Assemblies and Parliament at national level; and United Nations Oranization at the global level.

In the Indian society, the Christians are members of the *Kirk* but people of all faiths and no faith are citizens of *Polis*. Like the citizens assemble before their governor, Christians too assemble before their God. Both Kirk and Polis are similar by way of being communities constituted by people; yet both are different by virtue of being governed by different authorities; *Polis* by the government whereas *Kirk* by God. Let us first dwell on the subject of *Kirk* and subsequently on *Polis*.

Kirk

Kirk is constituted of God's people. In the north India context the church is a fragile community of broken (servile) and beaten (defeated) people i.e. *Dalit* and *Adivasi* respectively. They, like any other community require "order" *vyavastha*. By "order" we mean two things. The first is the *scheme-for-organizing* the community and second is the *policies-for-governing*. In "order" the scheme and policies are intertwined and are inseparable. But the scheme of order and the policies to govern a community can best be understood by understanding the beliefs *astha* of the adherents because the design to organize and the policies to govern their community are propounded by their religious belief *astha*. Admittedly different faith communities have different schemes of organizing their people. These orders are social arrangements which are either hierarchical or egalitarian. Our aim here is to understand the social arrangement *vyavastha* as propounded in the New Testament.

The gospels offer a *scheme-of-organizing* people into a community. This scheme is social equality or egalitarianism. Therefore, the task of the church is to advance equality to make all people free and equal citizens. Now the social design as propounded in the gospel is neither hierarchic nor monarchic nor oligarchic which are exclusivist by nature; it is egalitarian that is inclusive and just. Promotion of egalitarianism may not wholly stem out the differences but at least it values each person equally and thereby treats people with dignity. (Mt 12.48ff; 20.25-28; 23.8-12)

This takes us to the subject of *policies-for-governing* the community, which is another aspect of order *vyavastha*. The policy is democracy. Due to a greater possibility in democratic culture for people to intermingle, it has an appeal for the broken and beaten people. Intermingling means to have fellowship. The *Kirk* or church has to facilitate fellowship of the servile and defeated people by encouraging inter-dining, inter-marriages, mutual listening, public discussion and forging alliances. It not only unifies God's people who are broken and beaten, but unites them to Christ.

In this respect the phrase "rooted in soil and related to Christ", which in slight variation was coined by Bishop Pritam Santram to describe salient features of the Church of North India, can also be used to describe the ideals for an Indian Church.

Rooted in Soil

James Massey, an eminent Dalit theologian, proposed and 'incarnational model' based on John and Luke that would cover the entire Dalit issues and is oriented towards the re-visioning of a Dalit community. St John wrote,

> "(The Word in flesh) came to that which was his own, but his own did not receive him. Yet to all who did receive him, to those who believed in his name, he gave the right to become children of God—children born not of natural descent, nor of human decision or a husband's will, but born of God.
>
> The Word became flesh and made his dwelling among us. We have seen his glory, the glory of the one and only Son, who came from the Father, full of grace and truth." (John1.11-14).

This model would see God dealing with the Dalit situation by himself becoming fragile human being, one who, according to Isaiah, "had no form or comeliness." (Isa. 53.4). This act of God brought God into complete solidarity with the Dalits. St Luke writes,

> "While (Joseph and Mary) were there, the time came for the baby to be born, and (Mary) gave birth to her first born, a son. She wrapped him in cloths and placed him in a manger, because there was no guest room available for them." (Luke 2.7).

God came down to earth, became a human being and was born to live among the poorest of the poor; God became fragile being i.e. a Dalit or untouchable, in order to make all Dalits of this world fully human and to flourish (2 Cor.8.9). God rooted himself to soil through his Word made flesh.

Related to Christ

Essentially what goes on in the *Kirk* or Church is something conceived by God, created by God and maintained by God, as St Paul wrote,

> "Christ loved the church and gave himself for her. That He might sanctify and cleanse her with the washing of water by the word, that He might present her to himself a glorious church ... holy and without blemish." (Eph. 5.25-26).

This mystic union makes the Church one with the body of Christ "his flesh and his bones" like wife and husband (Eph. 5.28-29). Therefore, if we affirm that Christ is just, then the Church, related to Christ as his espouse, should also be what Christ is. She too is ordered by justice, which is equality, freedom and fellowship.

I close this section of Kirk, by pointing out that Church is Christ's fragile community of Dalits and Adivasi i.e. servile and defeated people who are organized *vyavastha* according to their faith *astha* to flourish as free and equal people. For this being together and to flourish the important thing is friendship *maitri*, love *sneha* and fellowship *sangati*. Jesus had said to his disciples,

> "My command is this: Love each other as I have loved you. Greater love has no one than this: to lay down one's life for one's friends. You are my friends if you do what I command. I no longer call you servants, because a servant does not know his master's business. Instead, I have called you friends." (John15.12-15)

A genuine *Kirk* is a community of people who are bound together and welcome others among them with friendship, fellowship and love which includes compassion. The people of the *Kirk* are sisters and brothers. Such ethical values become practical when each member of the *Kirk* seriously relates to Christ as his sister or brother and friend.

Polis

Polis, or *Poleis* in plural form, is a Greek word which means *city*. In our times, as it was in the antiquity, city is an area where a large number of people live fairly close to each other. Perhaps an ideal paradigm for *Polis* could be a public park of a city. In a "Park Community" all citizens of the city enjoy with equal dignity the pleasures of natural beauty.

It is to such *Poleis* that people of all walks of life belong. They are called *citizens*. They decide to elect their city counsellors, decide their city matters. Each city has its own municipal councils for governance, and civic systems to provide transportation, and meet the needs of its *citizens* with regard to security, housing, food, sanitation, health-care, administration of justice and entertainment. Each Polis, therefore, constitutes a political community.

However, a *polis* as a political community is not a homogeneous body; instead it is a differentiated entity. There are those who "govern" and the rest of the population is "governed"; at the same time there is a party to "oppose" the legislatures and policies of the ruling party. But this also is a reinforcement of inequality of the rulers over the ruled. What perhaps conceptually aims towards an equal-treatment-of-all-people is the principle of equality of all citizens under the law of the land. Two things that Dr Ambedkar had held about the State must at once be reiterated here: firstly that no law should be enacted in violation of human rights; and secondly, that the *Polis* or State cannot delegate powers to private persons to govern others.

Having said this it is important to emphasise that every citizen as a member of the political community of *Polis* is expected to be pro-active. There are reasons for this. Politics is directly connected with power. To organize life in a *Polis* the citizens are coerced to behave in a way which the State would wish. In other words whoever forms the government also assumes power. Now if those who assume power are the dominant castes, then their ideology will be the caste system or *chatur-varna-vyavastha*. They will reinforce social inequality to the advantage of the members of the dominant castes.

In order to overthrow their dominance and establish egalitarianism, Dalits and Adivasi need to acquire equal and opposite power in adequate measure. Such power can be gained by active political engagement. Dr Ambedkar knew the advantage of democracy for Dalits to gain political power. There were greater chances for Dalits to gain political power through free and fair elections, than by any other means. If in this engagement the Dalits would constitute majority and form a government, they could then ensure at least two things: *one*, that equality in every sphere could be advanced and inequality reduced to the minimum. *two*, that Dalits and other subalterns would be aided with compensations of reservations and scholarships to reverse inequality for the benefit of the Dalits.

At the end of this study a word of caution is needed. Communities—*Kirk* or *Polis* like Caste or family—can be oppressive and unequal where its members could be deprived of friendship, love and fellowship. Despite the attempts to recover the advantages of community-life in our times, we should not naively idealize them. For example caste system creates anti-social atmosphere. It is pointless to promote community as one antagonistic force pitted against another, in the Indian context it is largely touchables against untouchables in an ascending scale of hatred and descending scale of contempt. Similarly patriarchy turns family oppressive by silencing its women and giving them a secondary treatment.

It is therefore important to balance the significance of community with the importance of individual. It would do us well to recall Dr Ambedkar's point that individual is an end in him/herself; and that they have certain inalienable rights which should be protected by collective entities whether family, *Kirk* or *Polis*; and that none except a *polis* (or State) should govern them.

Having said this we still can hold that communities—*Kirk* and *Polis*—are the locus to nurture and shape the nature of people. Granted that people are born with some innate natural traits, but human behaviour, despite its natural traits, can be moulded or reshaped in a community due to the human capacity of volition. Community can be a hope for individuals to progress in their life. A community that enables this to happen is a Flourishing Community. In other words a *Flourishing Community* is not the one that merely survives by helping people to adapt and adjust to the changes in their social and natural environment but enables to shape and re-shape their social environment on the moral principle of Justice so that all people are equal and free and progressive in their communities.

Bibliography

[BAWS] *Writings and Speeches. Babasaheb Dr B.R. Ambedkar*, Volume-1 (1989) Mumbai.

[BHC] Brearley. H. C. 1965. *"The Nature of Social Control"*, In Joseph S. Rock st. Al. (Ed) *Social Control*, Affiliated East West Press: New Delhi.

[DM] Daniel. Monodeep, 2007. *Models of Leadership in the Indian Church: An Evaluation*, published in Studies in World Christianity Vol-13 Part-1. Edinburgh.

[DM] Daniel. Monodeep, 2016. *From People to Community.* New Delhi. ISPCK.

[DM] Daniel. Monodeep, *Society in India: Dr Ambedkar's Vision* (2019) ISPCK. New Delhi.

[EB] *Encyclopaedia Britannica* Volume1973) 20-) William Benton Publisher. Chicago.

[HYN] Harari. Yuvan Noah, *Sapiens* (2014) vintage. London.

[JG] Jacob. Godson, *Community in the Writings of Jürgen Moltmann for an Indian Ecclesiology* (2019) ISPCK New Delhi.

[MJ] Massey. James, 1994. *Towards Dalit Hermeneutics: Rereading the Text, the History and the Literature.* New Delhi. ISPCK.

[SA] Sen. Amartya, 2005. *The Argumentative Indian: Writings on Indian History, Culture and Identity.* London. Penguin Books.

[RAS] Rathore. Aakash Singh, *Ambedkar Preamble: A Secret History of the Constitution of India* (2020) Vintage Penguin Books. Gurugram.

[TR] Thapar. Romila, 2000. *Cultural Pasts: Essays in Early Indian History.* New Delhi. Oxford University Press.

[VK] Vanhoozer. Kevin J. (Editor), *Cambridge Companion to Postmodern Theology* (2003) Cambridge University Press. Cambridge U.K.

Index